BOB PEGG

RITES AND RIOTS

FOLK CUSTOMS OF
BRITAIN AND EUROPE

BOB PEGG

RITES AND RIOTS

FOLK CUSTOMS OF BRITAIN AND EUROPE

BLANDFORD PRESS

POOLE   DORSET

First published in the U.K. 1981 by Blandford Press
Link House, West Street, Poole, Dorset. BH15 1LL

Text copyright © 1981 Bob Pegg

British Library Cataloguing in Publication Data

Pegg, Bob
  Rites and riots.
  1. Folklore — Europe
  I. Title
  398′094   GR135

ISBN 0 7137 0997 9

Phototypeset by Oliver Burridge & Co. Ltd
Designed by Richard Johnson
Printed and bound by Hazell Watson & Viney Ltd., Aylesbury

Contents

Illustrations

A number of problems arose in captioning the illustrations for this book. Some illustrations are of uncertain origin and date but, wherever practical, an approximate date has been given. Early non-photographic representations of customs may be highly idealised, even purely imaginary, and many, particularly those from the nineteenth century, are as likely to be based on written accounts as on anything actually witnessed. Their value lies in the fantasies which they express, many of which we have inherited. It should be remembered that the earlier photographs may show uncharacteristic poses as a result of conventions of portraiture or limitations of equipment.

The following sources are gratefully acknowledged:

Black and white photographs
BBC Hulton Picture Library: pp. 17, 34, 35, 36, 41, 55, 70, 72, 74, 86, 93, 103 (top), 108, 121; Guy le Boyer/EFDSS: p. 99; C. Eric Brown/Doc Rowe Collection: p. 49; Cambridge Daily News/Doc Rowe Collection: p. 84 (top); EFDSS: pp. 24, 42, 76, 81, 100 (top); Gherlone/EFDSS: p. 92; Mary Evans Picture Library: pp. 22 (bottom), 28, 30, 51, 59, 65, 118, 123, 124; J. Kettleburgh/Doc Rowe Collection: p. 26; London Illustrated News/EFDSS: p. 82; George Long/Doc Rowe Collection: p. 103 (bottom); Martin Parr: p. 127; George Pickow/EFDSS: p. 22 (top left); Reuter/EFDSS: p. 23 (bottom); Doc Rowe Collection: pp. 23 (top), 27, 33, 38, 43, 44, 52, 91, 95 (top), 96 (top), 97 (top), 98, 100 (bottom), 101, 102, 139; S. Saulier/EFDSS: p. 22 (top right); I. B. Seougall/EFDSS: p. 96 (bottom); Brian Shuel: pp. 45, 47, 63, 84 (bottom), 97 (bottom), 128, 129, 130, 138; Sir Benjamin Stone/BBC Hulton Picture Library: pp. 57, 95 (bottom); Sir Benjamin Stone Collection/City of Birmingham Public Libraries Department: p. 64; Homer Sykes/Once a Year, Gordon Fraser: pp. 25, 60; Henry Taunt/Doc Rowe Collection: pp. 40, 90, 94.

Colour plates
Danish Tourist Board: 22; Mary Evans Picture Library: 23; Halcyon: 2, 16; Italian State Tourist Department: 1; Netherlands National Tourist Office: 10; Doc Rowe Collection: 4, 6, 7, 8, 12, 13, 18, 19, 21; Brian Shuel: 3, 5, 9, 14, 15, 17, 20; Homer Sykes: 11.

Acknowledgements

I WISH TO THANK David Bland, Ian Gibbs, Tony Green, and Bill Lloyd. While they may not necessarily share my opinions I would not have been able to write this book without their assistance.

Introduction

FACING THE DOUBTFUL, possibly non-existent future of a world which we did not choose to inhabit, and for which most of us feel no personal responsibility, members of literate, industrialised societies can easily look back in longing to a past when desire, ambition and social rank were more circumscribed, when children behaved themselves, when politicians and generals were great men, and when our ancestors were more in touch with both themselves and the natural forces that surrounded them and shaped their lives.

Hoping to contact this imagined past, we may buy any rural artefact, from a corn dolly to a country cottage, or we may escape once a week to the local folk club—to sing and play the popular music of nineteenth-century farm labourers—or join a Morris-dancing team, or revive local customs which died out in the early years of this century, or pay annual visits to similar customs which have lasted into the present.

If the past, however recent, is a series of fictions whose appeal is not at all diminished by our awareness of historical probabilities, one of the tales we like to believe is that popular folk or folk customs are survivals from a time when the members of a poor but contented peasantry, whose lives were rooted in the land they worked, celebrated the turning of the seasons and the accompanying vegetative cycle with simple jollity and innocent sexual licence. Or, if we are of a darker caste of mind, we may hold that old customs are debased forms of pre-Christian religious ceremonies, originally dedicated to fertility magic, human sacrifice, and the worship of dark gods.

In the following pages I have tried to separate record from fantasy, believing that readers will find the resulting picture of human behaviour as rich and as fascinating as any extravagant imaginings, however comforting or emotionally titillating those imaginings may be.

BOB PEGG

8

1. A passage through the wilderness

O N THE VILLAGE GREEN, which is lined with rows of thatched cottages that can have changed little in hundreds of years, a team of bearded Morris men leaps into the air. The dancers' white shirts and trousers are freshly laundered and the tiny bells strapped to their shins sparkle in the Spring sunlight. Near them, children, also clad in white, weave in and out around the Maypole, braiding the ribbons, which stream down from its apex, into a many coloured parasol. Later in the day, after the sun has gone down, you can hear the music of a song, a folk song so old that its origins are quite forgotten, drifting from the open upstairs window of a timbered coaching inn.

A vision of Old England which is not what it seems: for the Morris Dancers are teachers and university students, connoisseurs of real ale; the braiding of the Maypole was only introduced into England in the nineteenth century, long after raising a Maypole on the arrival of Spring had ceased to be a common feature of community life, and the singer is performing in the folk song club in the upstairs room of the inn, while the people in the public bar drink to the sound of the juke box.

Seen from this point of view, such efforts to mimic the popular culture of the past look like the doomed attempts of dissatisfied members of a technological society to recreate a Golden Age of bucolic contentment which never, in fact, existed. Superficially this is a reasonable analysis, yet it is by no means the whole truth about a situation in which, for several hundreds of years, literate and educated people have taken a fascinated interest in the rural and urban labouring-classes' predominantly seasonal celebrations, which are now called 'folk customs', themselves a part of the broader field of 'folklore', which includes, among other things, superstitious belief, music and songs, crafts, stories and legends.

The term 'folklore' was first coined, in 1846, by W. J. Thoms who, in a letter to *The Athenaeum*, was attempting to provide a focal point for the widespread interest in what had come to be called 'popular antiquities', which had concerned certain inquisitive writers, and accounts of which swelled the pages of a number of periodicals which had come into existence by the time Thoms was writing.

The antiquaries were fascinated by the past, often the past of the particular area in which they lived. Local legends and hearsay accounts were among the materials they used to create a picture of their chosen territory and, to get such information, as well as relying on previously published reports, they had to meet and talk with the people who lived there—a method of working the modern folklorist would call 'field-work'. Today the antiquary with whom we are most familiar is John Aubrey (1626–97). The familiarity comes from the theatre production, subsequently adapted for radio and television, of his collection of anecdotal biographies, *Brief Lives*, but Aubrey's interests ranged from the history of his native Wiltshire to ghosts and supernatural portents and his *Remaines of Gentilisme and Judaisme* (which was not published until nearly two hundred years after his death) contains many examples of what would now be called 'folk customs'.

In 1725, in Newcastle-upon-Tyne, *Antiquitates Vulgares; or, the Antiquities of the Common People*, by Henry Bourne, was published. Bourne, a Newcastle clergyman, was not simply presenting popular customs and beliefs as matters which would interest his readers. He saw nearly all folk belief as being 'either the Produce of Heathenism: or the Inventions of indolent Monks, who have nothing else to do', and similarly reckoned that some of the customs, while essentially beneficial, had retained 'little of their primitive Purity' and should therefore be rid of superstition, while others should be banned as 'a Scandal to Religion, and an encouraging of Wickedness'. So, for instance, the custom of drawing lots on St Valentine's Eve, to determine future marriage partners, was 'altogether diabolical' and, even if divorced from any accompanying superstition, it was still 'often attended with great Inconveniences and Misfortunes, with Uneasiness to Families, with Scandal, and sometimes with Ruin'.

Bourne shared this reforming attitude with earlier, Puritan, writers, notably Phillip Stubbes, from whom we shall hear later. His book stayed in obscurity until 1777, when it was republished in an expanded form by John Brand (1744–1806), another cleric from Newcastle, who, towards the end of his days, was to become the Secretary of the Society of Antiquaries in London. Judging by his 'General Preface', Brand had been irritated by the censorious tenor of Bourne's earlier work, but was nevertheless content to reprint it in its entirety, adding extra information and commentary, as *Observations on Popular Antiquities: Including the whole of Mr Bourne's Antiquitates Vulgares. . . .* Brand's attitude towards his materials was strikingly different from that of Bourne. Though he believed, as had many writers before him, that popular customs and beliefs had their origins in 'the Times when Popery was our established Religion', he was not interested in condemning them for that reason, but rather in tracing them back to their sources. At the same time he acknowledged, in a grand analogy, that such a search was largely condemned to fail:

> A Passage is to be forced through a Wilderness intricate and entangled: few Vestiges of former Labours can be found to direct us; we must oftentimes trace a tedious retrospective Course, perhaps to return at last weary and unsatisfied, from the making of Researches, fruitless as those of some ancient enthusiastic Traveller, who ranging the barren *African* Sands, had in vain attempted to investigate the Sources of the *Nile*.

In his desire to know where customs and beliefs came from, Brand presaged a widespread pre-occupation of later folklorists, a pre-occupation which still exists. In a later passage, he suggests that some defunct customs and pastimes should be revived at a time when 'the general Spread of Luxury and Dissipation threatens more than at any preceding Period to extinguish the Character of our boasted national Bravery'. (He refers to the fears of John Stow, the sixteenth-century antiquary, that suppression of outdoor customs may lead to 'worse Practices within Doors', a sort of reversal of the 'it keeps them off the streets' argument.) This reforming spirit was echoed specifically, nearly one hundred and fifty years later, in Cecil Sharp's attempt to give native folk music back to the English people, through the medium of the schools, so that their moral character should be improved; and generally in the hundreds of 'revivals' of customs—in this and the last century—which have produced phenomena like the Morris and Maypole Dancers who opened this chapter.

In his 'General Introduction', Brand, though referring to essentially the same information as did Bourne, supplants the latter's dogmatism with a reasonable tolerance and a spirit of historical enquiry which seems to look ahead to the nineteenth century rather than back to the times of religious intolerance and persecution.

At the time of his death, Brand was planning a new edition of the '*Popular Antiquities*' and, in 1808, the manuscript of this projected work was bought, by auction, by a group of fourteen people who entrusted it to the editorship of Sir Henry Ellis. Ellis was Keeper of Manuscripts at the British Museum and, as Brand had once been, the Secretary of the Society of Antiquaries. The book was finally published in two volumes, in 1813, as John Brand's *Observations on Popular Antiquities: chiefly illustrating the Origin of Our Vulgar Customs, Ceremonies and Superstitions*. It had become an unruly compendium of calendar customs, activities connected with the human life cycle, etymology, traditional games and superstitious beliefs, extending in the 1846 edition to over nine hundred close-printed pages. Richard Dorson, the American folklorist, claims that it 'laid the foundations for a science of folklore, and became a landmark in the history of English thought'.

Ellis' edition of Brand was greeted by an already alerted reading public, men who had money and time to spare, and who were often sufficiently divorced from the common people to find their customs as strange and absorbing as anything that might go on in a remote African village. They used the '*Popular Antiquities*' as a guide for their own enquiries, annotating their personal copies and contributing fresh information to publications like *The Gentleman's Magazine* and the various periodicals edited by William Hone, the London bookseller and pamphleteer. Poor people living in rural areas must have wondered what was going on when clergymen and well heeled gentlemen accosted them, demanding to know of old stories, ancient beliefs and traditional customs. The scene was set for Thom's proposal of 'folklore' as a marked-out field of serious study and for the formation, in England, in 1878, of the Folklore Society which is still in existence.

Over the preceding one and a half centuries and more, a growing search for national identity had produced enthusiasm for folk materials in countries besides England. Cultured interest in the doings of the peasantry was by no means a new thing even then, though depictions of them were likely to be patronising or idealised. The Elder Brueghel's paintings were not intended for hanging on cottage walls. Watteau portrayed the 'peasant chic' which was affected by the well-to-do French around the turn of the eighteenth century, where rustic dress and recreation were raised (or lowered) to the level of high fashion. Also in the eighteenth century, there was burgeoning interest in oral literature and peasant song, and Wordsworth and Coleridge were later to use the simple forms and language of old ballads in their attempt to reform English poetry. The Grimm Brothers' *Kinder- und Hausmärchen*, published in three volumes between 1812 and 1822, made people more fully aware of the tremendous vitality and richness of content of folk tales and legends and, in 1835, Jacob Grimm's *Deutsche Mythologie* established a broader and more scientific base for the study of old stories and superstitions. Walter Scott took a keen interest in antiquities and Thomas Hardy used folkloristic elements in his novels and stories. This 'outsiders'' interest has fed back information to the primary sources, so adding extra complexity to the folklorist's perennial search for origins.

In the nineteenth century, the partial acceptance of theories of evolution in the natural world was accompanied by a rise of similar theories of cultural evolution. In the past, origins of contemporary customs had been ascribed to the Jews, the Catholic Church, the Romans, Druids and so on, without there being much linking evidence other than obvious formal similarities. Now, in a great age of exploration, it was theoretically possible to study a much wider range of materials from all over the world and to work out, from more 'primitive' examples, the prime motivations whose meaning had often been lost in the customs of more advanced societies. The notion which became widely accepted, that European myths, legends and stories and, to a lesser extent, customs and beliefs, had their common origin in the early and hypothetical 'Aryan' race from which the Indo-European family of languages had evolved, was contested by E. B. Tylor (1832–1917). By observing worldwide similarities between the myths, beliefs and customs, in societies ranging from the savage to the civilised, he introduced the notion of 'survivals', notions and practices which arose naturally at a certain level in a society's development and lingered on, bereft of their essential meanings, among more sophisticated peoples.

Taking his lead from Tylor, and drawing heavily on Wilhelm Mannhardt's investigations into the agricultural customs of the European peasantry, James Frazer, in 1890, published *The Golden Bough*. Extended through later editions to twelve volumes, *The Golden Bough* presented such a vast amount of information about customs and beliefs that it served to bolster theories that were not Frazer's, and the work became so well known and discussed that one of its central motifs, that of ritual human sacrifice as a means of promoting agricultural fertility, stayed with us and helped to inspire poetry such as Eliot's *The Waste Land*, drama like David Rudkin's *Afore Night Come* and John Bowen's *Robin Redbreast* and popular novels such as *Harvest Home* by Tom Tryon. The idea also crops up periodically in the popular media, often in a report of some sinister rural murder accompanied by the hint that an isolated village community may still (secretly) be practising 'the Old Religion'. So, although folklore studies have developed different approaches since the last century, the popular idea is still of fertility rituals and human sacrifice.

Folklore writings no longer have the wide appeal that they had during the last century. The Folklore Society still exists quietly and a number of universities throughout the world have departments wholly or partly dedicated to the subject's study but their publications tend to be read mostly by other academics or by the relatively small number of self-funded individuals who conduct their own field research. To the casually interested, perhaps the most engaging feature of folklore is its air of mystery, the suggestion of something which has its roots in a distant and pagan past. It is this aspect which has helped *The Golden Bough* to retain its popularity (it was recently re-published as a glossy picture-book). But the demand for the enigmatic has been taken over by a popular enthusiasm for the occult (an enthusiasm which also gripped the Victorians), for subjects like flying saucers, fringe medicine, the I Ching and the Tarot, and so on. If another appealing aspect of folklore was the promise it gave to illuminate man's nature, this impulse too has changed direction and is now turned inwards towards a much more individualistic kind of self-knowledge, to be gained from activities like meditation and group encounter. General interest in folklore tends to treat it as a spectacle, or as an activity in which to join.

In 1634, some verses were published in which the writer, probably a man from Leeds, wrote with regret about the passing of old customs:

And you, my native town, which was, of old,
(When as thy bon-fires burn'd and May Poles stood,
And when thy wassall-cups were uncontroll'd,)
The summer bower of peace and neighbourhood.
Although since these went down, thou lyst forlorn,
By factious schismes and humours overborne,
Some able hand I hope thy rod will raise,
That thou mayst see once more thy happy daies.

Popular customs, like those the writer mentions, had been condemned by Puritans as Papal superstition, and have been suppressed at other times, and for other reasons, by civil authorities and by the Church, as we shall see later. But the customs were nevertheless extremely tenacious and continued to survive, revive, re-create and create themselves. By the time the study of folklore had become an accepted discipline, it was a matter of local and national pride to some folklorists that old customs should not be allowed to die out. It was felt that such customs should be given plenty of moral support and, if they had died out within living memory, they should be reconstructed and resuscitated. Hence the May Day celebrations at Padstow, in Cornwall, are invaded not only by tourists and television film teams, but by folklorists with cameras and tape recorders, while the ubiquitous Morris Dancer is in most instances a re-creation by the folk dance revivalists who went around at the turn of the century, noting steps from the few surviving teams and from the old men who remembered them from their youthful dancing days.

Such a situation presents problems for the folklorists. The constant interplay between themselves and their subject, the filtering-back into the general public's awareness of their discoveries and theories—through books, magazine articles, television and radio programmes and, of course, the folklorists' personal contact with 'the folk'—has produced a situation where it is very difficult to assess the true significance of the activities and beliefs the folklorists are looking at. There is, for instance, a BBC recording, made in the 1950s by Peter Kennedy, of two Somerset men, Walter and Harry Sealy, describing apple tree Wassailing. One of them, to explain why guns were fired into the trees, states that the purpose of the explosions is 'to drive the evil spirits out of the trees'. Such a bald statement of intent may seem the perfect explanation, implying that the custom has its origin in a primitive way of seeing the world, that it is a survival which has kept its inner purpose as well as its outer trappings intact. But how far can we trust such a conclusion? The idea of driving out evil spirits from the trees is certainly appealing, and just possibly may have been handed down through the community for hundreds of years, but it may equally have had its origin with some folkloristically minded person who donated it to the custom during the last century. We know, too, that, internationally, many customs, not just Wassailing, have been accompanied by the firing of guns. There may be some underlying, half-conscious feeling that to do so helps keep antagonistic elements at bay, but in many cases I think we need look no further than the exhilaration of popping off a gun—the same kind of exhilaration that an adolescent may feel when roaring about on a high-powered motor cycle—and the simple enjoyment of 'raising hell', like the bad cowboys in a Western movie, who ride into town with their six-guns blazing, scattering old women, children and dogs, and causing even grown men to run for cover.

It is because of such complexities and confusions that I have put off trying to define what, for the purpose of this book, is meant by 'folk custom'. Popular works on the subject tend to assume that they are dealing with a well defined field and simply list activities which are already accepted as belonging to that field. In this way, existing, if vague, notions of the nature of folk customs are perpetuated without being put under any scrutiny. We have inherited certain ideas about pagan ritual survivals, fertility ceremonies etc, and any bizarre activities which fit into this preconceived framework are fair game. For it is their strangeness, as much as anything, which has brought the customs to the attention of the folklorist in the first place. The customs, after all, came first and it was a growing awareness of their 'otherness', of the way they did not appear to fit in with the increasingly urbanised society in which they took place, that led people to try and study them scientifically and speculatively.

I have assumed that what we call 'folk customs' are activities which have been engaged in by certain groups of people, generally, though not exclusively, the urban and rural labouring-classes and the peasantry. Various lettered individuals have observed these activities and have recorded them, often not just for their own sake, but in order to use them to make some religious, moral, historical or educational point. Many groups of customs are undoubtedly attached to specific times of year and many contain elements which are irrational to the point of suggesting an underlying magical or religious basis which does not conform to the official established practices of the countries in which they take place. But my interest is not so much in the possibility of the survival of pagan ritual as in recognising that both the participants in the customs and the people who have recorded them were, and are, individuals with differing motives and points of view.

It is natural to accept accounts of customs as being essentially accurate, but we should be at least a little wary of accepting unquestioningly the information we have been given. Such information may, for instance, contain errors which result from a simple ignorance of regional dialect. The folklorist may be the victim of deceit, wittingly or otherwise. 'Informants', as the people who give the folklorist information are frequently called, are often keen to please and quick to see the motive behind a question. They may supply what they think is desired, as in the case of the Yorkshire Dales' singer who told me that a particular song was 'a good old local one', even though he had made it up himself, basing it on a traditional model. He wasn't lying, in the sense that the model was old (and widespread) and his version mentioned many local place names, but when I asked where he had learnt it he hedged around the answer. He was, in fact, being as obliging and hospitable as possible, but for many years I had the wrong impression of the song's origins. At other times people may simply withhold information to which they feel the folklorist is not entitled or they may give false information to lead

Bampton Morris with 'Jinky' Wells, Oxfordshire, 1947.

him off the track. I have heard a story, which of course may itself be false, that a certain team of Morris Dancers hoodwinked Cecil Sharp, by giving him the wrong steps and figures to their own dances. There was certainly trouble when 'Jinky' Wells, the fiddler for the Bampton Morris side, supplied Sharp with information. He was accused by other members of the side of 'selling the Morris'.

One of the greatest problems in assessing most early accounts of folk customs is that they tend to give only the antiquary's point of view. After all, to most observers the people they were looking at were simple and illiterate, unmindful of the true significance of the customs they had preserved. Why question them at length if they didn't understand the essential nature of what they were doing? So a folklorist is likely to emphasize aspects of a tradition which reflect his or her own interests or which fit in with preconceived ideas, while possibly ignoring or giving only passing mention to aspects which may, in fact, be of equal importance. One aspect which generally gets left out of accounts is, as I have implied above, the viewpoint of the participants themselves, e.g. why they indulge in a particular activity at a particular time of year or of their lives and what feelings they experience while doing so. And now, as I have also implied,

17

ideas deriving from folklore studies are so widespread that they may easily have become an integral part of the attitudes of the participants in a custom. So the folklorist is rather like a man staring at a scene in a mirror who must be aware, to fully understand that scene, that his own reflection is a major part of what he is looking at.

Having said this, it is also true to say that many contemporary students of folklore are fully aware of the problems which beset their enquiries. They have tried to act as impartial observers, while, at the same time, often getting to know their informants on quite intimate terms, so that they can assess more accurately the nature of the information they receive. Like true scientists they draw their conclusions by looking at available evidence, rather than selecting evidence which fits in with existing theories. Some have also looked away from the 'obviously' ancient and turned their attention to folklore where it thrives, in the social life of modern cities, in industry and sport etc. They may, for instance, end up looking at the lore of the motor car, or of popular music, and at customs which, though they have no hints of paganism, nevertheless have much in common with older activities which do. Many folklorists have gradually come to the conclusion that the materials of folklore are not necessarily a thing of the past, relics of ancient and outmoded ways of thinking, but the means by which people try to make sense of the world (or to confront its lack of sense) and to alleviate boredom and suffering. By following a similar line, I hope to show that folk customs, both today and in the past, possess functions which have made them of immediate value to the people who take part in them and to show that some contemporary activities which we take for granted have much in common with the more obviously exotic and intriguing activities which so engaged the searchers after 'survivals'.

2. The light months

IT IS A MISTAKE to assume that people living in other places and times have held the same attitudes towards the world and their place in it as ourselves. We know that they did not and do not. Take, for instance, the difference between the Chinese Taoist way of thinking and the modern Western approach to life. The Taoist sees the world as being in a process of continual decay and re-creation. Each phase contains within itself the seed of the next phase and the wise person does not try to combat adversity. Since the process of change is cyclic, he submits to the times as best he can, knowing that, eventually, things will alter to a more advantageous state. At the same time the latter situation will not last forever and, even while things are going well, he must prepare himself for the inevitable decline. Urban Europeans, on the other hand, are much more inclined to see their lives in terms of an evolutionary progression. If things are going badly, we should fight against them, battle them out, in order to try and alter our circumstances by effort. The strongest and the most able go to the top of the dung hill, while the weaker members of society have to put up with what is almost certainly a less congenial situation.

Similarly our attitudes towards the natural world change according to the kind of society in which we live. The countryside does not look the same today as it looked in, say, the eighteenth or the twelfth century. For a start there is less of it and it has been tamed and confined by increasing urbanisation, by the needs and greeds of industry and agriculture, and by the improvement of road systems. As more people go to live in towns and cities, they tend to use the countryside for recreation, somewhere to go for 'a change'. To urban people, for example, the weather is something that happens around them; it happens *to* country dwellers. The writer and critic, John Berger, in writing of peasant communities, says:

Peasant life is a life committed completely to survival. . . .

Inexhaustibly committed to wresting a life from the earth, bound to the present of endless work, the peasant nevertheless sees life as an interlude. This is confirmed by his daily familiarity with the cycle of birth, life and death. . . .

The peasant sees life as an interlude because of the dual contrary movement through time of his thoughts and feelings which in turn derives from the dual nature of the peasant economy. His dream is to return to a life that is not handicapped. His determination is to hand on the means of survival (if possible made more secure, compared to what he inherited) to his children. His ideals are located in the past; his obligations are to the future, which he himself will not live to see. After his death he will not be transported into the future—his notion of immortality is different: he will return to the past.

These two movements, towards the past and the future are not as contrary as they might first appear because basically the peasant has a cyclic view of time.

Bearing such problems of perspective in mind, how are we to assess the significance of activities which, for the past three centuries or so, have been interpreted variously as Druidic rites, fertility magic, ancient 'survivals' etc? It seems wisest not to draw definite conclusions at all, unless we hear directly from the people who take part in these activities—which we call 'folk customs'—and what their reasons are for taking part; and, even in cases where testimony to 'primitive' motives exists, we should be aware that we may be receiving secondary information rather than a direct expression of individual or group self-knowledge. Our safest course is to look first at the available information about what people *do*, to see what patterns and tendencies emerge and then, perhaps, to try and relate these patterns and tendencies to aspirations and urges which appear to be universal, however differently they may manifest themselves in different societies. We can assume, for instance, a reaction to seasonal change in the majority of people throughout the world, however muted such reaction might be. For example, a time of vegetable renewal may bring a feeling of relief that a life-sustaining crop is ensured or just a feeling of well-being and vitality corresponding with the natural tendency to revival. It is a time of change, the crossing of a threshold and, as we shall see, folk customs tend to cluster around such times, whether they occur in the lives of human beings or in the natural world around them.

In most European countries, the period preceding Lent, when Winter is on the retreat, is given over to the festival of Carnival. In earlier times, the celebrations lasted from Christmas and before, generally reaching a climax in the three days before Ash Wednesday, but more recently they have tended to last for shorter periods. Rodney Gallop, writing, from personal experience, in *Portugal: a Book of Folk Ways*, saw Carnival in decline there 'almost restricted in the capital to the wearing of fancy dress and to processions of decorated cars and carriages. . . .' He also points out, however, that it was not always such a tame affair. He quotes an early nineteenth-century account of the Lisbon Carnival:

'In the middling classes,' wrote A.P.D.G. in 1826 [*Sketches of Portuguese Life, Manners etc.*], 'the frolics of Carnival consist in throwing hair powder and water in each others' faces and over their clothes; and pelting the passengers in the streets with oranges, eggs and many other missiles besides throwing buckets of water on them.' In a later passage the same writer mentions small india-rubber squirts, stuffed gloves smeared with grease and chimney-black, dust, and wax water-bombs. . . . People organised 'assaults' on the houses of friends, and it is on record that in one such *assalto* on a popular actress living in the Rocio Square no fewer than six hundred eggs were used as missiles.

In the past, there have been attempts to outlaw some of the more disruptive aspects of Carnival; so, for example, the use of squirts and the pelting of people with rotten oranges were banned in Portugal in 1604 and, in 1689, the use of masks was prohibited. Disguise had allowed the undetected commission of numerous crimes and the settling of old scores, and there was a time when anyone caught wearing a mask during Carnival might expect to spend four years exiled to Angola. Even as late as the 1930s, visitors to private houses would often be plastered with a sticky mixture of flour and eggs, and the ubiquity of the telephone had instigated the revival of an old tradition called the *pulha*, once an open sexual jibe or insult between opposite members of the sexes, but reduced by modern communications to the level of the anonymous obscene telephone call. In the Portuguese provinces, fortunately, Gallop found the Carnival tradition in a more vigorous form 'with battles of flour, rotten eggs, oranges and wax water-bombs, with infernal serenades and cacophonic "rough music," with soot-blackened faces, with tilting on horseback at bags of filth, with *pulhas* which disdain the secret of the telephone'.

The spirit of Carnival has often been personified in the form of a man or an effigy. In *The Golden Bough*, Frazer tells of the activities in the Italian town of Frosinone on Shrove Tuesday, the last day of Carnival, when the nine-foot-high dummy which repre-

Carnival giants, Pamplona, Spain, 1953.

Tarasque and Tarascaires, Tarascon, France, 1946.

Salisbury Giant with Hob-Nob, Hampshire. From a photograph taken in 1887.

sented the festival was seated on a throne on a huge float, drawn by four horses. Bringing up the rear of the wild procession, the local policemen handed out free wine to anyone who asked for it and the celebrations ended in the town square, where the effigy was stripped of its finery and burnt.

Gigantic figures are still a feature of Carnival in many European countries: at Nice, in France, for instance, where traditionally they are built by members of a few artisan families, who have had the skill passed down to them from previous generations, and in Belgium, possibly the most Carnival-conscious country, where the giants who head the Shrove Tuesday procession are accompanied by the orange-carrying *Gilles* who wreak havoc among the crowds. Giants, incidentally, were also common in English civic and guild processions, as for instance at Salisbury, where a figure three times the height of a man, ferociously bearded and wearing a tricorne hat, walked out with the Tailors' Guild on public occasions.

People take advantage of Carnival to wear fantastic costumes and disguises which, as in Portugal, enable them to behave in ways which would not normally be tolerated. In Viareggio, in Italy, the festivities last from January to Shrove Tuesday and feature processions of celebrants who wear elaborate satirical masks. The *Hoûres* at Eben-Emael, in Belgium, wear two red and black striped skirts, one tied round the waist and the other round the neck. With their heads covered, and wearing veils, they chase the unwary with brooms or pig-bladders and mark two black lines on each of the cheeks of anyone they catch; and in Stavelot,

Gilles with baskets for offerings, Binche, Belgium.

Gilles with oranges, Binche, Belgium.

also in Belgium, Carnival is revived in mid-Lent by the fooleries of the *Blanc-Moussis*, who are dressed in white and wear white masks with red noses. At Arreçife, on Lanzarote in the Canary Islands, the streets are invaded by men with blacked faces, wearing women's clothes and jabbering in a nonsense language.

Carnival has been burned, cremated, shot, drowned and decapitated (with a realistic show of blood spurting from tubes in his neck) and sometimes mourned, as in Malta until 1737, where women, shrouded in black, carried his straw-stuffed linen body

Shrove Tuesday carnival figures, Rottweiler, Germany.

through the streets, wailing like professional mourners at the end of each verse of their funeral dirge. In the Ardennes, in the last century, *Mardi Gras'* symbolic death became reality when the man playing the part was shot accidentally by the traditional firing squad. This put an end to similar mock executions in the area. At Patras, in Greece, King Carnival is burnt in the main square, among firework displays and masked dancers. At one time in France, burial seems to have been common. The *Morning Chronicle* for 10 March 1791 noted that:

> The Peasantry of France distinguish Ash Wednesday in a very singular manner. They carry an effigy of a similar description to our Guy Faux round the adjacent villages, and collect money for his funeral, as this day, according to their creed, is the death of good living. After sundry absurd mummeries, the corpse is deposited in the earth.

Carnival is still buried in Germany. In the town of München-Gladbach, near the border with Holland, the official Carnival period, or *Fasching*, starts at eleven minutes past eleven o'clock on the morning of 11 November. In mid-February, there is a special Women's Day, when women disguise themselves as old crones and take possession of the Town Hall, to which the Mayor hands them the keys. After this they dance and sing in the streets and cut off the tie of any man they can catch. At last, on Ash Wednesday, Hoppiditz—the Spirit of Carnival—is buried and everyone goes out for a fish meal.

In England, the pre-Lenten customs were less boisterous than elsewhere, but this period was still a time of celebration and licence. A writer in *The Gentleman's Magazine* tells of the goings-on in a small east Kent village on the Tuesday before Shrove Tuesday in 1779:

> . . . I found an odd sort of sport going forward: the girls, from eighteen to five or six years old, were assembled in a crowd, and burning an uncouth effigy, which they called an Holly-Boy, and which it seems they had stolen from the boys, who, in another part of the village, were assembled together, and burning what they called an Ivy-Girl, which they had stolen from the girls: all this ceremony was accompanied with loud huzzas, noise, and acclamations. What it all means I cannot tell, although I inquired of several of the oldest people in the place, who could only answer that it had always been a sport at this season of the year.

In 1440, a man called John Gladman rode through the streets of Norwich on Shrove Tuesday as the King of Christmas, on a horse decorated with tinsel 'and other nyse disgisy things'.

Before him went representatives of the twelve months of the year, each dressed in a suitable costume, and among them was Lent, dressed in red and white herring skins, with a horse decked with oyster shells, as a sign that, now the season of merriment was over 'sadnesse shuld folowe and an holy tyme, and so rode in diverse stretis of the Cite with other people with hym disguysed, making myrth, disportes, and plays etc'.

Shrove Tuesday Skipping, Scarborough, Yorkshire.

Shrove Tuesday is also a time for sport. The traditional sport of the day is Football, going back at least to the twelfth century, and still played in a few places. In its hey-day it bore little resemblance to the modern sport. Goals, which were often natural features of the landscape, were sometimes miles apart and many members of a community or of opposing communities would take part. Huge crowds formed round the ball and brute force as much as skill won the day. In France, northern England and Scotland, the opposing sides were often the bachelors and the married men of the parish—sometimes the married women and the spinsters.

In England, the Pancake Races of the Midlands are of recent origin and the only widespread surviving Shrove Tuesday custom is the making and eating of pancakes, an activity which once helped to 'stock up' the body in preparation for the

25

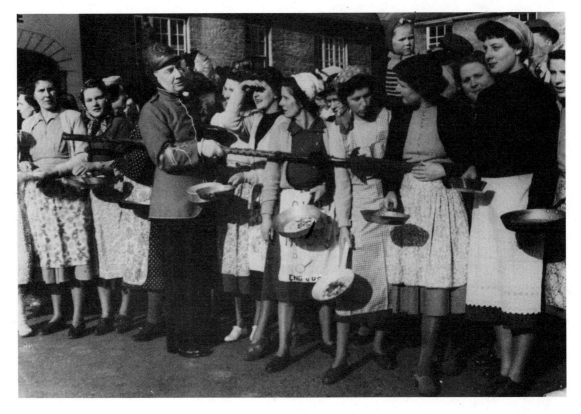

Olney Pancake Race,
Buckinghamshire, 1950s.

austerities of Lent and is now purely a source of gastronomic pleasure. John Brand tells how, in Newcastle-upon-Tyne, on Fasten's E'en, the bell of St Nicholas' Church tolled at mid-day (Pancake Bells were once common and still ring in some places), all the shops and offices shut down abruptly, and the rest of the day was given over to 'a little carnival':

> The custom of frying Pancakes (in turning of which in the pan there is usually a good deal of pleasantry in the kitchen) is still retained in many families of the better sort throughout the kingdom, but seems, if the present fashionable contempt of old customs continues, not likely to last another century.

Brand was wrong to have misgivings about the durability of the practice and it may have become even more widespread, since he mentions that it was observed by 'families of the better sort'. This was certainly not the case within living memory in the mid-Pennines where, on Collop Monday, the day before Shrove Tuesday, children, who were often from the poorer families, would go around knocking on doors and asking of the woman of the house, 'Pray dame, a collop'. The collop was a slice of bacon cut from the whole side which might be hanging up to smoke in

Pancake Tossing, Westminster School, London. Mid 19th century.

the chimney. The fat from it would be used the following day to cook pancakes. In Switzerland pancakes are eaten not on Shrove Tuesday but on the Thursday, *Schmutzig* or Fat Thursday, the day when Carnival begins in most of the Catholic areas.

Shrove Tuesday was also a general holiday for children and apprentices. The pastime of Throwing at Cocks with sticks was extremely popular with boys on that day and went on at least until the end of the eighteenth century, although it was dangerous (a thirteen-year-old boy was killed in Leeds in 1783) and widely condemned as a barbarous sport.

It was also common on Shrove Tuesday for children to shut their teachers out of school, a custom known as Barring-Out the Master. In the parish of Bromfield, in Cumberland, in the eighteenth century, the master was kept out for three days, as the children barricaded themselves inside the school, defending it 'like a besieged city', with pop-guns. If the master managed to re-assert his authority, he did so on his own stringent terms, but

Throwing at Cocks. A fanciful interpretation, c.1850.

he was usually defeated and, after the three days were up, a general agreement would be reached, and signed, by master and pupils, as to the terms of work and recreation at the school during the following year. One privilege the children always gained was immediately to hold a cock-fight and then a football match.

In Bromfield, the custom of Barring-Out the Master died out in the same century, but Peter and Iona Opie—in *The Lore and Language of Schoolchildren* (1959)—say that it continued in Tideswell, in Derbyshire, at least until 1938, though, since by that time the day had become a local holiday, the whole business was something of a pretence. Lawlessness of other kinds has, however, persisted into this century. The evening of Shrove Tuesday is a Mischief Night in Ireland, one of those times of the year when children can pester older people under cover of darkness, and the Opies report children with blacked faces going around the farms on Exmoor and in the Brendon Hills on Shrove Tuesday and on the previous evening demanding:

Tippety, tippety tin,
Give me a pancake and I will come in.
Tippety, tippety toe,
Give me a pancake and I will go.

If they could get into a house undetected they would throw broken crocks over the floor and sneak out again. This was once a common practice in the south of England and an account from the eighteenth century has a similar custom in the Scilly Isles of boys throwing stones at their neighbours' doors on Shrove

Tuesday evening. 'I could never learn from whence this custom took its rise', says the writer, 'but am informed that the same custom is now used in several provinces of Spain, as well as in some parts of Cornwall. The terms demanded by the boys are pancakes, or money, to capitulate'.

Mid-Lent, the fourth Sunday in Lent, is Mothering Sunday. Commercial interests working behind the once-independent Mother's Day, established by a Philadelphia woman after the death of her own mother in 1906, have given fresh impetus to a custom which has been going on quietly for at least three hundred years in rural places. There is passing reference to it as early as 1644 and, by the end of the eighteenth century, it had reached the general attention of the enthusiasts for antiquities. In 1784, a correspondent with *The Gentleman's Magazine* announced that he first came across the custom when staying the previous year near Chepstow:

> My enquiries into the origin and meaning of it were fruitless; but the practice thereabouts was, for all servants and apprentices, on Mid-Lent Sunday, to visit their parents, and make them a present of money, a trinket, or some nice eatable; and they are all anxious not to fail in this custom.

In some countries, mid-Lent is the time for the Carrying-Out of Death, a custom similar, if not identical, to the burning, drowning, shooting etc of Carnival. Among young people of Bohemia, says Frazer, the practice was for a puppet named Death to be cast into water, after which a tree was cut down and on it was hung another puppet, representing a woman dressed in white. This was carried by the troupe from house to house as they collected money and sang songs interspersed with a refrain which went:

We carry Death out of the village,
We bring Summer into the village.

Frazer holds that the puppet, or in some places a living person, was a 'representative of the tree-spirit' and adds that 'the "Summer" is the spirit of vegetation returning or reviving in spring', but these are plainly his own interpretations rather than the beliefs of the people who took part in the custom.

If we stop to look at the customs which have already been mentioned, certain common features will already be apparent. Perhaps the most outstanding general feature is the strangeness of many of them, the elements they contain whose existence bears no rational explanation. While we cannot disregard these

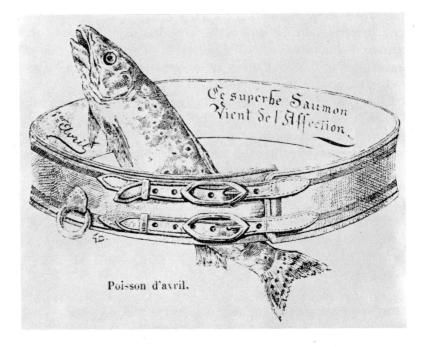

Poisson d'avril.

Poisson d'Avril.

irrational elements, we should bear in mind that they are one of the main reasons why the customs attracted attention in the first place and we should go on to consider how, in everyday life, we perform many irrational acts which are too ordinary to attract much attention, like knocking on a letter-box for luck after posting a letter or not stepping on the cracks in the pavement for fear of something terrible happening to us. We don't do such things for any particular reason, nor are they 'survivals' which have lost their true meaning. We do them because they *feel* appropriate and reassuring. (Of course, we can ask why we have such feelings, but any explanation is likely to be both speculative and unrelated to conscious motivation.)

Apart from this misleading strangeness, there are other things that many of the customs have in common. One striking factor is how often they involve begging for money and for food. While begging might not be tolerated as a general rule, it is permitted on specific occasions and (as we shall see later) the stingy are often rewarded with a curse from the beggars. Such breaks in convention, while apparently only an incidental part of some customs, seem to be a driving force behind many others. Carnival is a time when all rules are broken, or perhaps when new rules come into existence. A similar reversal takes place on 1 April, which is April Fools' or All Fools' Day (or, in Scotland, Huntigowk Day, for Hunting the Cuckoo). Usually only until mid-day, April Fools' Day is a time of trickery and deceit, when apprentices may be sent on pointless errands, like fetching a packet of bubbles for a spirit-level; where, in England, children mock the tricked one, crying 'April Fool', and, in France, the *Poissons d'Avril* have paper fishes pinned to their backs.

Easter is one of the main Church festivals, but it also has many customs attached which have no apparent connection with Christianity. One apparent exception is the Burning of Judas in the predominantly Catholic dockland area of Liverpool. There, at dawn on Good Friday, say the Opies, the streets are filled with children bearing effigies of Judas looking like a 5 November Guy Fawkes and, at sunrise, they pester people still asleep with, 'Judas is a penny short of his breakfast'. To get rid of them, the house-holders have to throw pennies out of the bedroom windows. Judases are then burnt on street bonfires, though many are carted off by the police. Poor Judas is also destroyed in Spain (it is said that the custom came to Liverpool from there), in Portugal and in the Latin American countries. He was once burnt in Germany too and his ashes planted in the fields on 1 May. Gallop notes that, in Portugal, 'the traitor is often clad in the blue over-alls of a mechanic and hung from telegraph wires'.

In the central north of England, Easter was, until recently, a time for the Pace-Eggers, or Paste-Eggers, to perform in the streets of towns and around the farmsteads of country areas. Groups of young men or boys enacted a drama of formalised battle, death and the revival of the dead by a comic Doctor. At the end of the short play, the boys (who generally wore costumes roughly appropriate to their roles—St George, the Black Moroccan Prince etc) took a collection of money or eggs. In parts of Cumbria and North Yorkshire, the Jollyboys went around dressed according to character—Lord Nelson, Lord Collingwood, the Heavy Young Lad, the Old Miser with Bags, and Tosspot—generally performing no play but singing a song which began:

Here's two or three Jollyboys, all in one mind.
We've come a Pace-Egging and we hope you'll prove kind.
We hope you'll prove kind with your eggs and strong beer,
And we'll come no more nigh you until the next year.

The egg had widespread associations with Easter and many countries still have customs incorporating eggs. There is the simple gift of a confectionary egg to a child, but real eggs have been begged, rolled down hills, smashed together like conkers, or hidden, as in Italy, where children have to hunt for their painted eggs in the garden. Before the introduction of confectionary eggs, most Easter Eggs were decorated in some way, by either engraving or dyeing. One way to decorate an egg is to draw a pattern on the shell with wax, wrap the egg in onion skins and boil it. When the egg is hard and cooled, remove the shell and the inscribed image is left white while the rest of the skin is stained a reddish brown.

The fact that the egg is linked with Easter in Christian countries has led to its being interpreted as a symbol of renewal representing the Resurrection. The Irish folklorist, Kevin Danaher, has a more functional explanation:

> Eggs are associated with Easter simply and solely, in my opinion, because according to regulation you did not eat them during Lent and because you had a superfluity of eggs by the time Easter came along.

He also believes that 'everything associated with Lent and Easter derives directly or indirectly from Christian custom and tradition and not from anything more ancient' since, in western Europe, 'there were no such festivals until the introduction of Christianity'. I would not entirely agree. The destruction of Lent and the Burning of Judas are echoed by the immolation of effigies at other times of the year. The Pace-Egg Play is directly related to very similar dramas which were more generally performed around Christmas and the New Year, and was itself a phenomenon which enjoyed greatest popularity in the nineteenth century; there is no strong evidence for the existence of any of these plays before the eighteenth century.

Another custom, now defunct, of Heaving or Lifting, at Easter, would require tortuous argument to link it to Christian belief. An account from 1787 describes how this largely northern English bit of fun was indulged in, on the Monday and Tuesday of Easter week:

> On the first day, a party of men go with a chair into every house to which they can get admission, force every female to be seated in their vehicle, and lift them up three times, with loud huzzas. For this they claim the reward of a chaste salute, which those who are too coy to submit to may get exempted from by a fine of one shilling, and receive a written testimony, which secures them from a repetition of the ceremony for that day. On the Tuesday the women claim the same privilege, and pursue their business in the same manner, with this addition—that they guard every avenue to the town, and stop every passenger, pedestrian, equestrian or vehicular.

In *The Gentleman's Magazine* for 1784, a Manchester writer suggested that the custom of Heaving was intended 'to represent our Saviour's Resurrection', but the connection seems tenuous,

Heaving, Easter, c.1800.

to say the least. Easter is not just a Christian festival, but also a public holiday. If we accept that apparently archaic activities (like the Pace-Egg Play) do not necessarily have their origins in the remote past and that, for many people, the Christian festivals were of little significance except to provide a respite from labour, then there is no reason to assume that every custom which took place during these festivals was linked, even indirectly, to Christianity.

The celebrations attached to the climax of Spring, around 1 May, were more unbridled than those of Easter and sometimes ran in to severe opposition from the Church and civil authorities. In London, in 1517, the suppression of May Day riots led to fourteen people being hanged, drawn and quartered and another four hundred-odd were saved from a similar fate when Henry VIII took pity on them, having met them face-to-face with the nooses already around their necks. Two years earlier the King himself had gone out Maying. When he and Queen Catherine reached the top of Shooter's Hill, they came across two hundred bowmen dressed in green with green hoods. Their leader, Robin Hood, asked the King if he would stay to watch the men shoot and, when this had been agreed, Robin Hood whistled and two hundred arrows were loosed simultaneously, each with a

Country Maypole, c.1750.

whistling device on the tip. After arrows had been shot a second time, the King and Queen were served in the greenwood with wine and venison by Hood and his men. Such well planned celebrations were not uncommon among the wealthy, but May customs were more likely to be of the unofficial kind, like those condemned by the Puritan writer Phillip Stubbes, in *The Anatomie of Abuses*, published in London in 1583:

> Against May, Whitsonday, or other time, all the yung men and maides, olde men and wives, run gadding over night to the woods, groves, hils, and mountains, where they spend all the night in plesant pastimes; and in the morning they return, bringing with them birch and branches of trees, to deck their assemblies withall. And no mervaile, for there is a great Lord present amongst them, as superintendent and Lord over their pastimes and sportes, namely, Sathan, prince of hel. But the chiefest jewel they bring from thence is their May-pole, which they bring home with great veneration, as thus. They have twentie or fortie yoke of oxen, every oxe having a sweet nose-gay of flouers placed on the tip of his hornes, and these oxen drawe home this May-pole (this stynkyng ydol, rather), which is covered all over with floures and hearbs, bound round about with strings, from the top to the bottome, and sometime painted with variable colours,

Elstow May Festival, Bedfordshire, 1951.

with two or three hundred men, women and children following it with great devotion. And thus beeing reared up, with hand-kercheefs and flags hovering on the top, they straw the ground rounde about, binde green boughes about it, set up sommer haules, bowers, and arbors hard by it. And then fall they to daunce about it, like as the heathen people did at the dedication of the Idols, whereof this is a perfect pattern, or rather the thing itself. I have heard it credibly reported . . . that of fortie, three-score, or a hundred maides going to the wood over night, there have scaresly the third part of them returned home againe un-defiled.

Stubbes' account is detailed but, presumably, generalised from a number of instances. (Note also, his claim that the visits to the woods, at least, took place at other times of the year as well as May.) He plainly did not witness the mass copulation of which he speaks and it is interesting that, three hundred years later, Frazer used Stubbes as one of his references when suggesting that 'we shall probably do no injustice to our forefathers if we conclude that they once celebrated the return of spring with rites which in their grossest form are said to be still observed in various parts of Holland at Whitsuntide'. This Spring/fertility/copulation series of associations has led to the general acceptance

Braiding the Maypole, Northfleet, Kent, 1949.

of the Maypole as a phallic symbol. So it is, to those who write and talk about it as such, but it is debatable whether it had such connotations to the people who took part in the May celebrations. From Stubbes' pre-Freudian point of view it was an idol, an object of religious worship.

On a more superficial level, we tend to see the Maypole as the quintessential symbol of Spring customs because it has been the centrepiece of so many village green revivals, and because it is such a striking *image* that illustrators, photographers and film-makers are naturally attracted to it. Its function has certainly changed, witness the contrast between the wild dance described by Stubbes and the disciplined, ribbon-plaiting children that we generally see today. And though some Maypoles were erected permanently, it is plain from many accounts that the decorated pole or tree is just one instance of vegetation brought into communities from the woods outside to celebrate Spring's arrival. Brand gives it as an Italian custom and also mentions an undated French source describing how, on May Eve, in the town of Commercy in Lorraine:

. . . beneath the windows of those for whom they bear affection, people plant young leafy trees, sometimes decorated with flowers and ribbons, which are called 'Mai.' This Mai is usually planted by a lover under his mistress' window or by pupils at their teachers' doors.

Occasionally a dead animal would be substituted for the Mai if someone had a score to settle. A certain vengefulness can also be seen in an account, published in 1867, of Maying in the Vosges Mountains, where girls went around from house to house on the first Sunday in May, singing a May song. If they received money for their efforts they would fasten a green bough to the door, but if refused they wished the family plenty of children and no bread to feed them.

Maypoles were banned in England during the Reformation, but they were never suppressed entirely. As late as 1660, one Puritan writer expressed his disapproval of the May celebrations in verse, describing the rascally crowd which convened round the pole:

Of fidlers, pedlers, jayle-scap't slaves,
Of tinkers, turn-coats, tospot-knaves,
Of theeves and scape-thrifts many a one,
With bouncing Besse, and jolly Jone,
With idle boyes, and journey-men,
And vagrants that their country run. . . .

He goes on to say that:

The most of these May-poles are stollen, yet they give out that the poles are given them. . . . There were two May-poles set up in my parish; the one was stollen, and the other was given by a profest papist. That which was stolen was said to bee given when 'twas proved to their faces that 'twas stollen, and they were made to acknowledge their offence. This pole that was stollen was rated at five shillings: if all the poles one with another were so rated, which was stollen this May, what a considerable sum would it amount to! Fightings and bloodshed are usual at such meetings, insomuch that 'tis a common saying, that 'tis *no festival unless there bee some fightings.*

This is just one of many instances in which the people taking part in customs have run into trouble. In countries which are predominantly Roman Catholic, however, the Church has generally been wise enough to incorporate as much as it can of native folk traditions into its own forms of worship. In *Spanish Fiestas* Nina Epton gives examples of such assimilation:

Engraving based on The Milkmaid's Garland, *by Francis Hayman, painted c.1735 for Vauxhall Gardens. The 'garland' is of plate rather than flowers.*

In Spain, the clergy has tried to channel these outbursts of [Springtime] eroticism and direct them to the spiritual sphere. *Mayos* are sung to the Virgin Mary rather than to the girl next door and in many localities the maypole is replaced by celebrations commemorating the discovery of the true cross by St Helena, on 3 May.

Many customs were kept up in urban as well as in rural areas. In the latter half of the eighteenth century, milk-maids danced with their garlands through the streets of London and, in earlier times, in the sixteenth century, Maypoles were set up in the streets and bonfires lit. Bonfires were commonly associated with May celebrations (as they were also with customs at other times of the year—we have already seen how effigies were burnt at Lent). In Celtic countries they were often called Beltane fires because of the corresponding seasonal festival of the same name. Here it was common for people to drive their cattle through the fires and the custom of people themselves jumping over the flames was common. In the volume of Sir John Sinclair's *The Statistical Account of Scotland*, published in 1794, the minister of

Callander, in Perthshire, describes what happened in his district at the May bonfires:

> ... all the boys in a township or hamlet meet in the moors. They cut a table in the green sod, of a round figure, by casting a trench in the ground of such circumference as to hold the whole company. They kindle a fire, and dress a repast of eggs and milk in the consistence of a custard. They knead a cake of oatmeal, which is toasted at the embers against a stone. After the custard is eaten up, they divide the cake into so many portions, as similar as possible to one another in size and shape, as there are persons in the company. They daub one of these portions all over with charcoal until it be perfectly black. They put all the bits of the cake into a bonnet. Every one, blindfold, draws out a portion. He who holds the bonnet is entitled to the last bit. Whoever draws the black bit is the devoted person who is to be sacrificed to *Baal*, whose favour they mean to implore, in rendering the year productive of the sustenance of man and beast. There is little doubt of these inhuman sacrifices having been once offered in this country as well as in the East, although they now pass from the act of sacrificing, and only compel the *devoted* person to leap three times through the flames; with which the ceremonies of this festival are closed.

In one giant mental leap, a children's game of forfeit becomes the remnants of pagan human sacrifice, though, as with similar accounts which speculate on the savage origins of customs, the children themselves have no notion of the 'survival's' real meaning.

Back in the city of London, the Ellis edition of Brand talks of another May spectacle:

> The young chimney-sweepers, some of whom are fantastically dressed in girls' clothes, with a great profusion of brick-dust by way of paint, gilt-paper, etc., making a noise with their shovels and brushes, are now the most striking objects in the celebration of May Day in the streets of London.

A young sweep might also don a costume of foliage to transform himself into a Jack-in-the-Green. These characters, supporting a wicker frame covered in greenery, survived in England into this century (and are rumoured to appear today in parts of Germany). The illustrator, E. H. Shepherd, in his biography, *Drawn from Memory*, recalls an encounter with a Jack-in-the-Green from his London boyhood:

> One fellow, completely covered with greenery, so that only his legs were showing, was jigging up and down. Another had his

Jack-in-the-Green, Oxford, May Day 1886. Revived about this time by Henry Hathaway, a chimney sweep and slaughterer.

face smeared with paint to represent a clown, and a third, in striped cloth coat and trousers, with a huge collar and a blackened face, was beating a tambourine. But the one that really frightened me was a man got up as a woman, in a coloured ill-fitting dress, a wig made of tow, and showing brawny arms above dirty white gloves. Brandishing a parasol, he, or she, held it out to catch coins thrown by passers-by or from the houses. . . . I never could bear to see the sight of a man dressed as a woman after that.

In Spring, figures like the Jack-in-the-Green made widespread appearances. In the nineteenth century in Brie, in France, for instance, a boy wrapped in leaves and called Father May, was a part of the May Day activities and, in Briançon, a jilted boy would be dressed up in green leaves by his companions and would then lie down on the ground pretending to be asleep. A girl who wished to marry him would rouse him and lead him to the ale-house, where the couple would initiate dancing. If the two were not then married within a year, the young people after that would have nothing to do with them.

Nina Epton tells of another May custom involving the idea of marriage, this time from twentieth-century Spain, where:

... at Manguilla in the province of Extremadura . . ., on the last night of April, a little boy and girl are chosen to represent a 'bride' and her 'groom'. The boy is dressed in his Sunday best by his mother and then he is led, followed by his parents and a crowd of villagers, to the house of his bride, carrying a branch of orange blossom decorated with buns. They knock at the house of the bride but the door remains closed while a dialogue is spoken by two adults, the one inside the bride's house representing a priest. Both parties find fault with the bride and groom but finally a marriage is agreed. Then the door is opened and the two children embrace; the little boy hands his decorated branch to the little girl and the villagers dance in the plaza.

May Queen and Maypole procession, Stratford-on-Avon, Warwickshire, 1914.

Many customs, like the one just recounted, centre round individuals who are chosen by the community or by the group which takes part in the custom. In Scotland an 'Abbott' was elected to preside over the May Day activities and I remember how, in the small Midlands town where I was born, the Band of Hope Union (an alliance of the Chapels who advocated temperance) organised a May Festival, which included a parade with floats through the streets after which people assembled in the local hall to watch the crowning of the May Queen, a girl who

May Queen and Garland, Glatton, Huntingdonshire. Mid 19th century.

was often a member of a prominent local family. The choosing of a May Queen was so common in the Alentejo and Algarve provinces of Portugal that each street had its own *Maia* and fighting between rival gangs of supporters occurred so frequently that the custom was banned in the 1870s. The election of May Queens was also widespread in France and in England. Frazer passes on an account from a domestic servant who had spent most of her life in the village of Stourton, in Warwickshire:

> . . . the Queen of May is still represented on May Day by a small girl dressed in white and wearing a wreath of flowers on her head. An older girl wheels the Queen in what is called a mail-cart, that is, a child's perambulator on two wheels. Another girl carries a money-box. Four boys bear the May-pole, a conical framework formed of a high tripod with a central shaft. . . . Each of the bearers has a garland of flowers slung over his shoulder. Thus the children go from house to house, singing their songs and receiving money, which goes to provide a treat for them in the afternoon.

Similarly, at Whitsuntide in Holland, poor women would go around begging, accompanied by a wagon in which sat a little girl wearing flowers and herself called the Whitsuntide Flower. In both the above instances it is worth pointing out that, whatever deeper symbolic significance might have been invested in the little girl, her innocence would also incite sympathy among the onlookers, so helping the process of the traditional redistribution of wealth that accompanies so many of the customs at which we have been looking.

The most remarkable surviving May Day celebrations are

Obby Oss, Padstow, Cornwall, 1910.

probably those held in the Cornish harbour town of Padstow. Towards the end of April, a Maypole is set up and the town decorated with flags and greenery. Sometimes during this period, crowds will congregate after the pubs have shut and spontaneous singing breaks out, but the official celebrations begin when a church bell strikes midnight on May Eve whereupon the people assembled outside the Golden Lion Inn strike up with what is called the 'Morning song'. They then perambulate around stopping at various houses and singing appropriate verses to the occupants. The main attraction at Padstow May Day, and the thing that draws thousands of tourists, is the Obby Oss, a heavy construction built around a six-foot-diameter hoop, covered in black canvas and supported on the shoulders of a man whose head is covered by a grotesque mask resembling a bishop's mitre in shape. In fact there are two such horses—with their respective teams—and numerous smaller versions worn by children. To the musical accompaniment of squeeze-boxes and drums, the horse performs a swaying, dipping dance, egged on by its Teazer, a man who wields a decorated club. The music dies and the horse

Sailor's Horse, Minehead, Cornwall, c.1914.

sinks to the ground, while the Teazer strokes it sensuously. Then suddenly the horse bounds up, the music revives and the Oss party carries on down the street to repeat the performance further along the route.

Padstow May Day is beloved of folklorists and its significance as a Spring fertility survival has been much discussed, together with the apparently impenetrable meanings of the songs that accompany it. The earliest known record of the celebrations dates from as late as 1803 and this is probably not written from first-hand experience; although the horse is an exotic, crowd-pulling figure, its appearance in May is exceptional, leading folklorists to suggest that it is a Christmas horse which has somehow changed season.

It seems remarkable that activities which were once so widespread but are now largely defunct should still be going on so vigorously at Padstow, which, while having for so long been an object of outside attention, has failed to succumb to the blandness and inoffensiveness which marks the purely tourist attraction.

E. C. Cawte, in *Ritual Animal Disguise*, gives possible reasons for this lively endurance:

> May Day at Padstow is the day of the year, the day when exiled Padstonians return home if they can, and it combines the merits of Christmas with the family, a Bank Holiday on Hampstead Heath, and a school reunion. There is also the awareness that Padstow is special, that people come from other parts of the country to see something that only Padstow can show, though in recent years the size of the crowd has been a matter for local regret.

Helston Furry Dance: main dance. Cornwall.

A Hobby Horse also appears around 1 May at Minehead, in Somerset, not far from Padstow, but it is virtually ignored by tourists and, apparently, by the majority of the Minehead people. However, at Helston in Cornwall, the May celebrations attract similar attention to those at Padstow. The dancing of the top-hatted men and their partners, who are dressed in white, has often been televised and the popular song, 'The floral dance', was inspired by the custom. It was described back in 1790 by a correspondent with *The Gentleman's Magazine*, who creates a picture of community involvement similar to that which E. C. Cawte ascribes to Padstow:

In the morning, very early, some troublesome rogues go round the streets with drums, or other noisy instruments, disturbing their sober neighbours, and singing parts of a song, the whole of which nobody now recollects, and of which I know no more than that there is mention in it of 'the grey goose quill', and of going to the green wood to bring home 'the Summer and the May-o.' And, accordingly, hawthorn flowering branches are worn in hats. The commonalty make it a general holiday; and if they find any person at work, make him ride on a pole, carried on men's shoulders, to the river, over which he is to leap in a wide place, if he can; if he cannot, he must leap in, for leap he must, or pay money. About 9 o'clock they appear before the school, and demand holiday for the Latin boys, which is invariably granted; after which they collect money from house to house. About the middle of the day they collect together, to dance hand-in-hand round the streets, to the sound of the fiddle, playing a particular tune, which they continue to do till it is dark. This they call a 'Faddy'. In the afternoon the gentility go to some farm-house in the neighbourhood, to drink tea, syllabub etc., and return in a morris-dance to the town, where they form a Faddy, and dance through the streets till it is dark, claiming a right of going through any person's house, in at one door, and out at the other. And here it formerly used to end, and the company of all kinds to disperse quietly to their several habitations; but latterly corruptions have in this, as in other matters, crept in by degrees. The ladies, all elegantly dressed in white muslins, are now conducted by their partners to the ballroom, where they continue their dance till suppertime; after which they all faddy it out of the house, breaking off by degrees to their respective houses. The mobility imitate their superiors, and also adjourn to the several public-houses, where they continue their dance till midnight. It is, upon the whole, a very festive, jovial, and withal so sober, and, I believe, singular custom. . . .

One noteworthy aspect of this account is the clarity with which it makes plain the differing behaviour of the upper and lower orders, so that the 'gentility', partakers of syllabub and tea, took part in the unusual dance (which, incidentally, gave them the opportunity to look around other people's houses), while the common people, troublesome rogues all, while having to content themselves with dancing through the streets, nevertheless made a nuisance of themselves with their early morning May song, forced people to jump in the river, begged money and, in the evening, imitated 'their superiors', appropriately in the pubs rather than in the ball-room.

At Whitsuntide—a holiday generally given over to sports and games—foliate figures appeared, similar to those we have already

Cheese Rolling, Cooper's Hill, Brockworth, Gloucestershire.

seen emerging at other times in Spring. In the last century, for instance, at Röllshausen in Germany, following the afternoon service on Whit Sunday, the children would go to the wood and cover one of their number, a boy, in greenery until he was unrecognisable. Then they went round from house to house, two of the boys leading the Little Whitsuntide Man, while two couples of girls carried a basket, singing and collecting eggs and cakes; in some places along the Rhine in Bavaria, a foliate youth called the Quack was led from door to door accompanied by singing and begging.

The Whitsuntide-lout at Fricktal, in Switzerland, was another boy covered in greenery, who was led through the village on horseback with a green leaf in his hand, until, at the village well, he was taken down and dipped in the water. It was then his turn to sprinkle everyone else and gangs of urchins would queue up for the privilege of being drenched. (Something similar happens today at the water festivals in Indonesia, where whole communities get soaked by hosing and by buckets of water.)

In southern England, one of the most prominent Whitsuntide customs was the Whitsun Ale, a feast generally organised by the Church, to which people from the parish, and sometimes people from neighbouring parishes, would come. It was a time when communities could get together and consume the food and drink that all had contributed and, after the feast, the younger ones would take part in dancing and sports while the elders looked on. In more recent times, chapels in northern England organised Whit Treats for their Sunday Schools along similar lines. On Whit Monday, the children would be taken out into a field, where they would have games like skipping, handball and foot-races—and sometimes dancing—and then be given something to eat.

Francis Douce (1757–1834) describes how it was customary to elect a Lord and Lady of the Ale at Whitsun Ales:

> Two persons are chosen, previously to the meeting, to be the lord and lady of the ale, who dress as suitably as they can to the characters they assume. A large empty barn, or some such building, is provided for the lord's hall, and fitted up with seats to accommodate the company. Here they assemble to dance and regale in the best manner their circumstances and the place will afford; and each young fellow treats his girl with a riband or favour. The lord and lady honour the hall with their presence, attended by the steward, sword-bearer, purse-bearer, and mace-bearer, with their several badges or ensigns of office. They have likewise a train-bearer or page, and a fool or jester, drest in a party-coloured jacket, whose ribaldry and gesticulation contribute not a little to the entertainment of some part of the company. The lord's music, consisting of a pipe and tabor, is employed to conduct the dance.

In Silesia, according to Frazer, the Whitsuntide King might be a youth who had won a horseback race to the Maypole. He was then raised by his companions and removed the garlands from the top of the pole. The worst rider, appointed the Clown, was meanwhile at the inn, consuming thirty rolls of bread and four quarts of brandy. The others, led by the King, arrived eventually at the inn and, if the Clown had finished his feast, the King had to pay his expenses. Otherwise the Clown (assuming he had survived the massive intake of food and alcohol) had to foot the bill himself. Later in the day, after the church service, the King headed a procession followed by the Clown, who by this time had his clothes on inside out and wore a false beard and a Whitsuntide crown. At each farmhouse they passed, the Clown was shut in while two guards demanded money of the housewife to wash the Clown's beard. They also made off with any food or drink that was not locked up. Eventually the procession came to the house of the King's girl-friend, the Whitsuntide Queen, who was given a sash, a cloth and an apron. The King received equivalent presents and also the honour of setting up the May-bush from the top of the Maypole in front of his master's house, where it stayed for exactly a year. Then the procession returned to the inn, where the King and Queen led off a dance.

Most of the more elaborate Whitsuntide customs have died

Garland King, Castleton,
Derbyshire, c.1950?

out. In Holland, however, Whitsun Brides appear in odd places and, in the same country at Whit, there is the practice of casting a straw effigy, called Lazybones, into the water, which is similar to some of the Lenten customs we have looked at. Children also fasten rubbish to the doors of people who have lain late in bed.

Oak Apple Day, 29 May, is also Garland Day in Castleton, in Derbyshire, and the accompanying custom has some features in common with Silesian Whit custom described above. The Garland itself is a three-foot-high wooden frame, decorated with leaves and bunches of wild flowers, and it is carried on the shoulders of the Garland King, who is mounted on horseback. The King is led through the village, with the Queen—also on horseback immediately behind him—and followed by a silver band and a group of girl dancers dressed in white. The procession stops at St Edmund's Church, where the Garland is taken off the King and hauled to the tower's highest point. Then the girls perform the Castleton Morris Dance in the market place to the music of the band. In *The Ancient Customs of Derbyshire*, Crichton Porteous declares that the custom is claimed 'to be unique'. All the customs we have looked at so far are unique in the sense that none exactly resembles the other, but at the same time all have elements which they share in common with other customs, and Castleton is no exception. For instance, until quite recently, the Queen was a youth dressed as woman, the rationalisation of this being that no woman would be able to control a horse among the music and the noise of the crowds (though later a woman did the job quite adequately). The man supporting a foliage-covered frame, the horseback ride around the village, the positioning of the Garland in a prominent place, and the dance (though here ceremonial rather than communal) are all features we have seen before. The usual explanation given for the existence of Garland Day is that it celebrates the Restoration of Charles II and the King, in fact, wears a Stewart costume. Porteous, on the other hand, suggests that 'it may have begun as a fertility rite, usually held on May Day'. This is possible, although such an explanation must always remain speculative. On the other hand the custom may in truth have started at the Restoration—when prohibition of such activities started to slacken off —perhaps using appropriate elements from customs which already existed in the surrounding area.

Ascension Day in Derbyshire marks the official beginning of the Well-Dressing, where wells in various villages in the Peak District are decorated with elaborate floral pictures representing scenes from the Bible. Water plays a part in many customs and wells were visited not only for simple decoration, but often to perform various ceremonies: people drank the water or immersed themselves in it to cure diseases and madness; they threw in pins to restore weak eyesight; they left rags hanging on nearby trees; and there is an instance, in eighteenth-century Wales, of a cock or a hen being sacrificed at one curing ceremony centred round a well.

Well-dressing is said to have been introduced into Derbyshire by an Italian priest, but decorating wells at Springtime was once a common and widespread activity. Flower decorations are themselves a natural accompaniment to the seasonal celebrations and some festivals are specifically dedicated to them. Palermo, in Italy, has one such festival in late May and early June and, also in June, there is a Battle of Flowers in Ventimiglia. In May, in all the main towns of Cyprus, there are floral parades, commonly held in stadiums, with chariots decorated to depict scenes from everyday life and from Greek mythology.

A number of the customs we have looked at so far include a bonfire as part of their make-up. Many festive occasions have inspired people to light up a fire, probably as much for excitement and warmth as for any ulterior reason, but Midsummer is a

Leaping across St John's Bonfire in Alsace, 1830s. By Thomas Schuler, 1863.

time of year which is particularly associated with huge blazes. Midsummer Eve (or the Eve of the Feast of St John) is a particularly popular time for bonfires. In some places in Denmark a 'witch' is burned on 23 June in the fires that spring up along the coast, and there are bonfires on the same evening in Finland, too, where people stay up all night celebrating. Similarly, in Norway, the Midsummer fires are accompanied by dancing and firework displays; and at Alicante, in Spain, wood and cardboard figures are burnt and bullfights held, while at San Pedro Manrique young men walk barefoot through the fires carrying passengers on their backs. In the Wachau district of Austria, in a miniaturised fire custom, egg-shells containing lighted wicks are floated down the Danube. In Ireland, according to Seán Ó'Suilleabháin, Midsummer bonfires are still lit in some places and, in earlier times, burning reed-sheaves were carried to encircle farms while a blackened sod from the bonfire was placed in the milk-house for good luck. The Irish, apparently, believed St John's Eve to be one of those times of the year when the door to the world of supernatural beings opened and people had to try and ward off the resulting danger. An account published in 1723 tells how:

On the vigil of St. John the Baptist's Nativity they make Bonfires, and run along the streets and fields with wisps of straw blazing on long poles to purify the air, which they think infectious, by

Burry Man, South Queensferry, Scotland, c.1960.

believing all the devils, spirits, ghosts, and hobgoblins fly abroad this night to hurt mankind.

On one occasion, at Whiteborough in Cornwall, a demon *did* appear on the tumulus where the Midsummer bonfire was lit. The Ellis edition of '*Popular Antiquities*' tells how:

> . . . I learnt at that place in October 1790, there was formerly a great bonfire on Midsummer Eve: a large summer pole was fixed in the centre, round which the fuel was heaped up. It had a large bush on the top of it. Round this were parties of wrestlers contending for small prizes. An honest countryman informed me, who had often been present at these merriments, that at one of them an evil spirit had appeared in the shape of a black dog, since which none could wrestle, even in jest, without receiving hurt; in consequence of which the wrestling was, in a great measure, laid aside. The rustics hereabout believe that giants are buried in these tumuli, and nothing would tempt them to be so sacrilegious as to disturb their bones.

Finally, before we enter Autumn, looking back at the green men who made such frequent appearances in Springtime, it is worth noting a similar figure who comes out later in the year. In South Queensferry, Midlothian, 4 August is the time of the Ferry Fair and, on the previous day, the Burry Man makes his seven miles' walk of the Queensferry boundaries. He is a strong man or youth who wears a wreath of roses on his head, while the flannel costume that covers his body is stuck with a mass of the prickly burrs which grow locally. The two staves that he carries in either hand are decorated with flowers and, because the costume is tremendously heavy, two ordinarily dressed men support him on his journey, which begins at nine in the morning and ends, with periods for rest, past tea-time in the afternoon. The attendants take a collection at the usual house-stops and the party divides the money between themselves to spend at the Fair the following day.

The custom is extremely unusual, if not unique, for the time of the year at which it takes place, and for the main ingredient of the costume, though of course it has the common elements of disguise (the Burry Man is unrecognisable since the costume covers the head as well as the body), the perambulation and the collecting of money.

3. The dark months

IF WE LOOK at many of the images and artefacts which accompany the customs of Spring it becomes plain that they reflect or embody the spirit of that season. Foliate and floral decoration, green humanoid figures, even the leaping of the Morris Dancers, all suggest traits which are physically and psychologically linked to the season itself. Whether or not any of the customs had their origins in fertility rituals, they are also direct responses in celebratory mimicry to a particular time of the year which promises revitalisation and sustenance. So it is not surprising that similarly appropriate customs are to be found in the Autumn, at harvest time. Today the response in England to this gathering-in is limited largely to the Christian Harvest Festival—which is not to deny the impressiveness of the altar displays of fruit, vegetables and grain—but in times before the intensive mechanisation of farming, the customs that accompanied the harvest were generally quite unrelated to the doings of the Church.

A great number of customs were connected with the last day of harvest and, specifically, with the last sheaf to be bound up. This sheaf was often given human form, dressed up or made into a doll, and it went by various names in different countries. Frazer says, for instance, that the commonest name in Germany for the last sheaf was the Corn-mother—though, there and in other countries, it also tended to be named according to the specific crop, Wheat-mother, Rye-mother etc—and other names include the Old Woman, the Bride, the Witch or Hag, the Child, the Bastard. Sometimes two effigies would be made at the same time so that, for instance, in parts of Scotland, the Old Wife might consist of the first stalks cut, and the Maiden of the last. The farmer would keep the Maiden but would pass on the Old Wife to a neighbour who had not fiinished his reaping and he, in turn, would pass her on to another tardy neighbour. The ultimate possessor would be the slowest farmer in the district and, as a

Harvest Supper, Cornwall.

Harvest Home, Last Sheaf,
Cornwall. Late 19th century.

55

forfeit, he might have to give some of his own grain to the community later in the year. In Pembrokeshire, the Hag was plaited from a small quantity of the last corn, which was cut by means of the reapers throwing their sickles at the last patch left standing in the harvest field. Then an emissary, usually the ploughman, would sneak unseen up to a neighbouring farm where work was still in progress and throw the Hag among the harvesters, ideally to land on the foreman's sickle. He then made good his escape as quickly as possible, since the angry workers were liable to send their sickles flying after him. Elsewhere, one of the reapers would take the Hag back to the farmhouse without being seen. If caught, he was often stripped and drenched with water specially reserved for his wetting, but if he got away with it he might receive a small amount of money or a jug of the best ale. Afterwards the Hag was hung up somewhere around the house and kept for the following year, as were some May garlands. Such year-long display was a common fate for many of these corn figures, though, in the Isle of Islay, the Old Wife was fed to the plough horses on the first day of ploughing, while in other places the last sheaf might end up in the possession of someone who, it was consequently reckoned, would be married within the year. Yet again, around Auxerre, in France, after a harvest dance where the fastest reaper and the prettiest girl danced around the last sheaf, which had been placed in the middle of the dance floor for the purpose, the sheaf itself was pulled to pieces and incinerated. Something similar still goes on in Poperinghe, in Belgium, on the first Sunday in September, where, at the end of the hop harvest, an effigy of Hommelvent, the Hop-man, is burnt.

In some places, people were wrapped in the last sheaf, so that, in Cracow, in Poland, the woman to bind the last sheaf was enfolded by it with only her head left visible. She was then carried to the house on the last harvest wagon, soaked by the family and left bound until the evening dance was over. For the subsequent year she kept the title of Baba, the Old Woman. Frazer mentions a custom in West Prussia where a boy was bound in the last sheaf and the resulting figure called the Bastard. The woman who bound the last sheaf then pretending to be going into labour and an old woman acted as midwife to her. When the phantom child had been delivered, the boy in the sheaf began to cry like a baby; he was then wrapped in a sack and taken to the barn to prevent him catching cold.

Frazer sees these end-of-harvest practices together with those of Spring, as 'based on the same ancient modes of thought, and [forming] parts of the same primitive heathendom, which was doubtless practised by our forefathers long before the dawn of

Kern Baby, Whatton,
Northumberland, 1902.

history'. He takes them to be reminiscent of magical rites, 'ceremonies which . . . are believed to influence the course of nature
directly through a physical sympathy or resemblance between
the rite and the effect which it is the intention of the rite to
produce'. The unanswered question remains as to what degree
the people taking part in the customs were conscious of such a
motive, even assuming that Frazer's suggestions are correct.
Some confusion arises from the fact that, though the last sheaf
itself is ubiquitous and can therefore be considered of some significance, the actual nature of the significance changes from
place to place. So the last sheaf may be connected with court-
ship, marriage or producing a child; and the first or last sheaf
may bring good luck to a farmer or may be used to bring bad
luck (or shame) to another farmer. The multiplicity of names

given to the last sheaf also suggests a great diversity of significance.

Again, Frazer has it that 'the Corn-mother ... is believed to be present in the handful of corn which is left standing last on the field', so that Hanoverian reapers would send her packing by beating the last sheaf, children were told not to pull poppies in the field or the Corn-mother would get them and when the wind runs through the crop in Spring:

> ... the peasants say, 'There comes the Corn-mother', or 'The Corn-mother is running over the field', or 'The Corn-mother is going through the corn'.

What is not clear is the degree to which such reactions testify to any real belief in a corn-spirit. Warning children that the Corn-mother will catch them is as good a way as any of protecting the crop from their trampling little feet and need not have been any different from the threat that 'the bogey-man will get you'. Similarly, we might say that 'Jack Frost was out last night' without implying any conscious belief in a frost spirit.

In giving most of his attention to the apparent marks of primitive ritual magic on harvest customs, Frazer only hints in passing at the general, and totally appropriate, air of celebration which was attached to that important time of the year. There are, however, other accounts which correct this imbalance. In *The Twelve Moneths*, published in London in 1661, M. Stevenson tells how:

> The Furmenty Pot welcomes home the Harvest Cart, and the Garland of Flowers crowns the Captain of the Reapers; the battle of the field is now stoutly fought. The pipe and the tabor are now busily set a-work; and the lad and the lass will have no lead on their heels. O 't is the merry time wherein honest neighbours make good cheer, and God is glorified in his blessings on the earth.

From the volume of *The Statistical Account of Scotland*, published in 1797, comes a description of harvest customs in the parish of Longforgan, Perth, which again places more emphasis on the fun that people had at harvest time:

> It was, till very lately, the custom to give what was called *a Maiden Feast*, upon the finishing of the Harvest; and to prepare for which, the last handful of Corn reaped in the field was called *the Maiden*. This was generally contrived to fall into the hands of one of the finest girls in the field, was dressed up with ribands, and brought home in triumph with the music of fiddles or bag-

Harvest Home, Poland.

pipes. A good dinner was given to the whole band, and the evening spent in joviality and dancing, while the fortunate lass who took the Maiden was the Queen of the Feast; after which this handful of Corn was dressed out generally in the form of a Cross, and hung up with the date of the year, in some conspicuous part of the house.

It is plain from these accounts that the elements in harvest customs which immediately attract folklorists are in no way divorced from the customs' celebratory aspects, but are inseparably linked to them. So the harvest cart is accompanied by musicians, while the harvest dance generally takes place in the presence of the last-sheaf effigy.

After the intense activity of harvest time the next important period in the customs calendar is the time around 31 October, when the idea of the dead returning home to eat and drink was once widespread throughout Europe. Even today, Hallowe'en has a strong grip on the popular imagination and *Hallowe'en* was an appropriately evocative title for a recently successful film by John Carpenter, in which a murderous lunatic with supernormal strength returns to terrorise his home town on that evening.

Punky Night, Hinton St George, Somerset.

Hallowe'en was, and still is, a time for divination, when a girl might, for instance, stand before a mirror at midnight and comb her hair three times, hoping to see the reflection of her future husband staring over her shoulder. Customs for this time of the year are generally kept up by children rather than adults. The Opies determined a border south of which Hallowe'en meant little, though, to the north, celebration was widespread. It stretched from 'somewhere around the mouth of the Humber south-west to Knighton, and then southwards along the Welsh border, counting Monmouthshire in with Wales, and then—although this line is less certain—south again through Dorset'. Games like bobbing for apples—trying to take a bite out of an apple floating in a butt of water—are still fairly common, and so is the Hallowe'en lantern, a swede or turnip hollowed out, with the features of a face or other designs cut in the skin and lit from inside by a candle.

For the Celtic people, 1 November was Samhain, the beginning of their New Year, and the previous evening was one of great activity, generally centring round the lighting of bonfires. This was common until quite recently. In *The Statistical Account of Scotland*, the minister of Callander in Perthshire tells how the people in his area celebrated this time of the year:

LEFT
1 Masked carnival figure, Sardinia.

BELOW
2 Clowns on stilts in procession at the annual fair, Verona, Italy.

3 Obby Oss and Teazer in the streets of Padstow, Cornwall, on May Day.

4 Garland Day, Abbotsbury, Dorset: children bearing one of the garlands around the village.

5 Well-dressing, Tissington, Derbyshire: pressing petals into a clay base.

FAR LEFT
*6 Well-dressing, Tideswell,
Derbyshire: completed picture.*

LEFT
*7 November 5th Celebrations,
Lewes, Sussex: Cliffe Bonfire
Society in torchlight procession.*

BELOW
*8 November 5th Celebrations,
Lewes, Sussex: burning effigy on
the bonfire, accompanied by
fireworks.*

LEFT
9 Garland King Day, Castleton, Derbyshire: a celebration of the Restoration of Charles II.

BELOW
10 St Nicholas and Black Peter arriving by barge, Amsterdam, Netherlands.

OVERLEAF
11 Mari Lloyd, Bridgend, Wales: a Midwinter horse.

On All Saints' Even they set up bonfires in every village. When the bonfire is consumed, the ashes are carefully collected into the form of a circle. There is a stone put in, near the circumference, for every person of several families interested in the bonfire; and whatever stone is moved out of its place or injured before the next morning, the person represented by that stone is devoted, or *fey*, and is supposed not to live twelve months from that day . . .

Writers of general accounts of folk customs tend to emphasise the fact that bonfires were once lit at specific times of the year. Midsummer Eve and Hallowe'en are often singled out but, as we have seen already, fire has played a part in many customs throughout the year. So, for instance, a correspondent with *The Gentleman's Magazine* for 1784 describes how:

. . . at the village of Findern, in Derbyshire, the boys and girls go every year in the evening of the 2d of November (All Souls' Day) to the adjoining common, and light up a number of small fires amongst the furze growing there, and call them by the name of *Tindles*.

Disguise is common at this time of the year. Among children, the Opies note the use of soot, paint and masks, as well as dressing-up in the clothes of the opposite sex. They tell how, in Scotland, children go around in groups calling themselves 'Guisers', often with blackened faces, begging money or food from houses. There is similar begging on 2 November, All Souls' Day, or on the previous day, when children in rural Cheshire and adjoining areas travel about the farms singing songs like:

Soul! Soul! for a soul-cake!
I pray you, good missis, a soul-cake!
An apple, a pear, a plum or a cherry,
Or any good thing to make us all merry.
One for Peter, two for Paul,
Three for Them that made us all.

A version of this song was recorded in the 1960s by the American 'folk' trio Peter, Paul and Mary and, for a while, it became popular in folk music clubs throughout England, perhaps leading to a revival of the custom in some places. According to the Opies, the children are given other gifts in place of Soul-cakes, which are no longer made, but still refer to the food and money they receive as 'Soul-Cakes'. Distribution of cakes of various kinds was once common on Hallowe'en. According to

61

The Gentleman's Magazine for 1790, housewives in Ripon, in Yorkshire, made cake for each member of their families, to be eaten on what was called 'Cake Night', and, in Warwickshire, Seed Cake (made 'at the end of wheat seed-time') was consumed. In Portugal, at the same time of the year, Rodney Gallop says that children went around singing hymns and asking for 'bread for God' and:

> At Cintra there is a tradition that nothing a child asks on this day may be refused. The carollers are rewarded either with a *magusto* or with *bolos de festa*, special cakes of sugar, cinnamon and sweet herbs.

In her book *Spanish Fiestas*, Nina Epton recounts:

> In the province of Zamora, especially in the village of Benavente, women bake special bread 'for the souls' in November. . . .
> In the month of November, either associated with All Souls' day on the 2nd, or with a patron saint . . . the Galicians hold fiestas called *o magosto*: communal picnics, consisting chiefly of chestnuts which ripen at this time of the year. . . . The fire is the important thing, into which the chestnuts are poked until they burst open. Boys and girls run after each other blackening their faces with the smokey exterior of the chestnuts.

In parts of Cheshire, a Souling Play was performed and, at Antrobus, there is a still extant version, which was revived in the earlier years of this century. The plays, preceded by a begging song, were followed by the appearance of a Wild Horse and his Driver. The Driver was sometimes dressed as a huntsman, while the horse was made of a horse's skull supported on a pole by a man who was covered with sacking or a horse-blanket. The horse was decorated with ribbons, horse-brasses etc, had a moveable jaw, which could be made to clack, and was sometimes given leather ears and the bottoms of bottles for eyes. E. C. Cawte describes the antics of the horse at Antrobus:

> The wild horse and his groom enter, the horse clashing his jaw, rearing, banging his pole on the floor, and making sallies into the audience. While this is going on the groom tries to calm him, and then proceeds in all seriousness, pausing only to calm the horse again as he rears and bangs each time he is spoken to.

In northern England, 4 November is a Mischief Night for children, as was May Eve in earlier times. During the course of this evening, children play tricks which would be less tolerated at other times of the year. In addition to more harmless pranks—

like tying together the doors of a terraced row of houses or rapping on windows with a button tied on a long piece of thread —lighted fireworks are pushed through letter-boxes and gates removed from their hinges to be floated on a pond or set drifting down a river. According to the Opies, Hallowe'en is a Mischief Night on Exmoor and also in Sutherland and Caithness, places geographically remote. Gates are again removed and, in northern Scotland, people's property is switched around, so that, for instance, on the morning of 1 November, a man might find a white horse in his stable where, the previous night, there had been a black one.

Antrobus Soulers, Cheshire.

The mayhem on Mischief Night in the north of England is accompanied by increasing activity connected with the following night, Guy Fawkes Night. In the area in which I live, the West Yorkshire Pennines, the evening of 5 November is known as 'Plot Night', presumably after the Gunpowder Plot, though the bonfires themselves are also referred to as 'plots'. There is much rivalry between the various groups of children, who prowl around in packs, dragging back to their own particular plots any piece of combustible material they can lay their hands on. Children sometimes take it in turns to guard their bonfires, as sabotage is common, with plots removed piecemeal to another site during the night or simply ignited by members of rival gangs.

Guy Fawkes Celebration, Windsor, Berkshire, 1899.

Effigies of Guy Fawkes are hauled around from house to house and the parties beg money for fireworks. I have seen at least one Guy who was a real boy in disguise.

In the 1841 edition of '*Popular Antiquities*', both John Brand and, in a note, Henry Ellis, imply that the 5 November bonfires were on the decline. If this was so, the custom has now gained in strength to the extent where, short of legislation intervening, it looks as if it will continue for a long time to come. Commercial interests, the selling of fireworks and masks, may have helped a revival—though they are surely more a response to a demand than instigators of that demand—but it is interesting to note how many features of customs we have already looked at have attached themselves to, or grown out of, the 5 November celebrations, specifically the bonfire itself, the destruction of an effigy and the ubiquitous begging. Since Guy Fawkes Night is not a particularly old tradition, and since it appears to have revived at a time when comparable customs were dying out, we can assume not only that the apparently archaic elements in 5 November customs have no direct link with a pagan past, but that they have

Raising the Bird Pole, Norway.

functions which appeal directly to young people (and many older ones) in an industrialised contemporary society. In other words, Guy Fawkes Night is not a 'survival', but it has so much in common with customs which are assumed to have direct links with primitive rites, that we may begin to ask ourselves to what extent the archaic activities we have observed are, in fact, recurring manifestations of general unconscious principles which are triggered off when people respond to various needs, impulses and external stimuli.

Christmas is now one of the major Christian feasts of the year, but it was by no means the first to be established. Before the fifth century, there was no general agreement between theologians and ecclesiastical authorities as to whether Christ's birth had taken place on 25 December, 6 January or 25 March, or even whether it was proper to celebrate the Nativity at all, whatever the correct date. Eventually, and not without dispute, the Church fathers decided on the time of the Winter Solstice, to which 25 December approximates, as being an appropriate date. This may have been no arbitrary decision. One of the policies of the early Church was to use elements of existing paganism rather than to try and stamp out utterly non-Christian religious practices in the territories it hoped to convert. Sending out missionaries from Rome in AD 601, Pope Gregory I ordered them to destroy idols, but to consecrate the temples in which they were found, and to replace heathen animal sacrifices by celebrations more appropriate to Christianity. The solstices were important in the religious practices of many of the potential converts and, in Britain, for instance, 25 December had, according to Bede, been observed as a 'mothers' night' and the beginning of a new year, before the arrival of Christianity. Whether or not any Christmas customs of the last few hundred years have direct links with the pre-Christian world, few of them seem to have much specifically to do with the birth of Christ. One exception, perhaps, is the giving and receiving of presents, but this practice was also a feature of the Roman Saturnalia and does not necessarily take place on Christmas Day, as is the case in England. In parts of Scotland, Wales, and the Border Counties, children go round to their friends and neighbours on 1 January, collecting gifts and food. If they call after mid-day they are dubbed fool, as are late tricksters on 1 April. At one time, the Christmas and New Year period was generally given over to the bestowing of gifts, not only between friends and family, but also between householders and those who provided them with services. We still talk of 'Christmas Boxes' and stories are told of disgruntled dustbin men who leave a trail of rubbish after having been refused a Christmas gratuity. The Frenchman, Misson de Valbourg, talks of this practice in *Memoirs and Observations in his Travels over England*, published in France in 1698, and translated into English in 1719:

> From Christmas Day till after Twelfth Day is a time of Christian rejoicing; a mixture of devotion and pleasure. They give treats, and make it their whole business to drive away melancholy. Whereas little presents from one another are made only on the first day of the year in France, they begin here at Christmas; and they are not so much presents from friend to friend, or from equal to equal (which is less practised in England now than formerly) as from superior to inferior. In the taverns the landlord gives part of what is eaten and drank in his house, that and the two next days; for instance, they reckon you for the wine, and tell you there is nothing to pay for bread, nor for your slice of Westphalia.

In many countries, children are brought their presents at this time of the year by St Nicholas, the Christian saint who was born in the third century, became a bishop and was renowned for giving unexpected gifts. In Germany, on the eve of 6 December, children put out boots in front of their doors and the following morning find them filled with sweets. Later in the day, their parents will take them along to a hall to see St Nikolaus, who has with him Knecht Ruprecht, a man with a blackened face, who brandishes a chain menacingly and carries a sack in which to put naughty children. In Amsterdam, on the Saturday before 6 December, St Nicholas arrives by boat from Spain (where, paradoxically, there is no Father Christmas) and rides through the streets on a white horse, on which he is also said to ride over the roof-tops. With him he brings Black Peter, a little black boy who distributes gifts to the children who are watching the procession. On the previous evening the children leave out a pair of clogs for Black Peter and carrots or hay for St Nicholas' horse.

In Spain itself, presents are brought not by St Nicholas but by the Three Wise Men and, in the mountainous regions of the north, the equivalent of Knecht Ruprecht is a little man made of paper and called *Fumera*, 'the Smoky One', who, hung by parents from a beam near the fireplace, watches the behaviour of children with his seven eyes on behalf of the Wise Men, who bring the presents on 6 January.

In some countries, for instance Germany and Italy, Christmas Day is kept as a solemn religious occasion, with the giving of presents confined to other times. In England, however, it has become a largely secular feast and often religious activity is confined to watching church services on television through a haze of alcohol and tobacco smoke. From the eleventh to the seventeenth century in England, Christmas became increasingly the great celebration of the year and it is not surprising that it was banned by Act of Parliament in 1644. Charles II restored the feast, however, and it appears to have revived well enough. In the past, gastronomic excess was even more pronounced than it is today. Misson describes one fantastic item which we no longer have on our tables:

Every family against Christmas makes a famous pie, which they call Christmas Pie. It is a great nostrum, the composition of this pastry: it is a most learned mixture of neats'-tongues, chicken, eggs, sugar, raisins, lemon and orange peel, various kinds of spicery etc.

Christmas, however, was not just a time for exchanging gifts and filling the belly. In 1811, *The Gentleman's Magazine* printed an account of Christmas activities in the North Riding of York-shire which shows just how busy a time of the year it was:

Here, and in the neighbouring villages, I spent my Christmas, and a happy Christmas too. I found the antient manners of our ancestors practised in every cottage: the thoughts of welcome-coming Christmas seem to fill the breast of every one with joy, whole months before its arrival. About 6 o'clock on Christmas Day, I was awakened by a sweet singing under my window; sur-prised at a visit so early and unexpected, I arose, and looking out of the window I beheld 6 young women, and 4 men, welcoming with sweet music the blessed morn. I went to Church about 11 o'clock, where every thing was performed in a most solemn manner. The windows and pews of the Church (and also the windows of houses) are adorned with branches of holly, which remain till Good Friday. From whence this custom arose I know not, unless it be as a lasting memorial of the blessed season.

Happy was I to find that not only the rich, but also the poor, shared the festivity of Christmas; for it is customary for the clergyman and gentlemen to distribute to the poorest people of their own village or parish, whole oxen and sheep, and to each a pint of ale also. Such was the hospitality of our ancestors; would that such customs were still practised among us!

In the North Riding of Yorkshire, it is customary for a party of singers, mostly consisting of women, to begin, at the feast of St. Martin, a kind of peregrination round the neighbouring villages, carrying with them a small waxen image of our Saviour, adorned with box and other evergreens, and singing at the same time a hymn, which, though rustic and uncouth, is, neverthe-less, replete with the sacred story of the Nativity. This custom is yearly continued till Christmas Eve, when their feasting, or as they usually call it 'good living', commences. Every rustic dame produces a cheese preserved for the sacred festival, upon which, before any part of it is tasted, according to an old custom, the origin of which may easily be traced, she, with a sharp knife, makes rude incisions to represent the cross. With this, and furmity, made of barley and meal, the cottage affords uninter-rupted hospitality. A large fire (on Christmas eve) is made, on which they pile large logs of wood, commonly called 'yule clog'; a piece of this is yearly preserved by each prudent housewife: I have seen no less than thirty remnants of these logs kept with the greatest care.

On the feast of St. Stephen large goose pies are made, all of which they distribute among their needy neighbours, except one which is carefully laid up and not tasted till the Purification of the Virgin, called Candlemas.

On the feast of St. Stephen also, 6 youths (called sword-dancers, from their dancing with swords), clad in white, and bedecked with ribbands, attended by a fiddler, and another youth curiously dressed, who generally has the name of 'Bessy', and also by one who personates a Doctor, begin to travel from village to village, performing a rude dance, called the sword-dance. One of the 6 above-mentioned acts the part of king in a kind of farce which consists of singing and dancing, when 'the Bessy' interferes while they are making a hexagon with their swords, and is killed. These frolicks they continue till New Year's Day, when they spend their gains at the ale-house with the greatest innocence and mirth, having invited all their rustic acquaintance.

There is in this part of Yorkshire a custom, which has been by the country people more or less revived, ever since the alteration in the Style and Calendar: namely, the watching, in the midnight of the New and Old Christmas Eve, by Bee-hives, to determine upon the right Christmas, from the humming noise which they suppose the bees will make when the birth of our Saviour took place. Disliking innovations, the utility of which they understand not, the oracle, they affirm, always prefers the more antient custom.

Another strange custom also prevails: that those who have not the common materials of making a fire, generally sit without one, on New Year's Day; for none of their neighbours, although hospitable at other times, will suffer them to light a candle at their fires. If they do, they say that someone of the family will die within the year.

This lengthy account was submitted to *The Gentleman's Magazine* by one R.S., who claimed that it was from the journal of a deceased friend, D-D R-E. Assuming that the whole passage is not faked, its ingenuous tone makes it of particular interest. D-D R-E appears to be an outsider, both socially and geographically to the area he describes. He has a vague notion that the events he has witnessed have their roots in the distant past—'the antient manners of our ancestors'—but seems unlikely to have had any broad antiquarian knowledge. Had this been the case, we might reasonably have expected him to work within a broader field of reference; the 'yule clog', for instance, merits several pages of information and speculation in John Brand's 1777 edition of '*Popular Antiquities*' (I am assuming D-D R-E wrote after this date).

As well as being widespread at Christmas time, many of the activities to which D-D R-E refers have broadly much in common with customs which have taken place at other times of the year, in other countries and in other circumstances. The 'peregrinations'—in this case of the carol singers, the effigy bearers, and the Sword Dancers—are a prominent feature of many customs we have already looked at, as is the collection of money (did the

Waits, Brittany. A fanciful cartoon. Late 19th century.

Mistletoe Gathering, Normandy, 1876.

carol singers and the people with the wax Jesus also collect?).
Customs connected with fire, together with taboos on lending it,
were also widespread. The use of greenery for decoration is
common at other times of the year, and plays and dances,
generally performed by groups of men, were not confined to
Christmas and the New Year.

Of the many activities described by D-D R-E, carol singing still

70

continues unabated. The carol, as a popular song dealing with a religious topic, is said to have had its origin in thirteenth-century Italy and to have passed from there to France and Germany, and then on to England. While many of our Christmas songs were written quite recently, some of the most popular have been taken from oral tradition and bear the marks of simplicity and repetition characteristic of folk songs. 'The holly and the ivy' and 'I saw three ships come sailing in' are well known examples. While the singing of these songs is now confined to Christmas, this would not always have been the case and some carols have a down-to-earth ring which has precluded their use in Church services, One, 'The cherry tree carol', has the elderly Joseph suspicious at Mary's unexpected pregnancy. She asks him to pick her some of the fruit from a cherry tree, but he sourly tells her to get the child's father to gather them. At this point Jesus' foetus speaks up from inside Mary's womb and orders the cherry tree to bow down its branches so that Mary may pick the cherries herself. There is a similar idea in a Spanish carol from Galicia, where:

St Joseph was jealous
When he saw that Mary was pregnant.
In His mother's womb
The Divine Child smiled.

The Yule Clog mentioned by D-D R-E, often known simply as the Yule Log, was a large piece of wood, brought into the home to burn conspicuously on the Christmas fire. Yule is the old Scandinavian celebration of the Winter Solstice—eventually becoming confused with Christmas time—and the Yule Log was supposedly disseminated by the Norsemen on their travels. It was still common in the north of England in the eighteenth century. D-D R-E says that the people in his unspecified area of the North Riding of Yorkshire kept the remnants of their Yule Logs. He gives no reason why this should be, though perhaps in Yorkshire, as in other places, a new log was lit with the remnants of the previous year's log. In some parts of the Scottish Highlands, a log was carved into human shape and burnt under the name of the Old Wife (one of the names given to the harvest effigies we looked at earlier). At Christmas in northern Spain, a hollow log, known as Uncle, is placed near the fire. He is treated with great reverence and filled with presents for the children, who beat him to see what will fall out. In Tuscany, the Christmas log is shaped into the form of a small hut. Speaking about Lorraine, an account from the *Mémoires de l'Académie Celtique* of 1809 reads, in translation:

Yule Log Blessing, Touraine.

On 24 December, around six o'clock in the evening, every family puts a huge log, called *the Christmas root*, on the fire. The children are forbidden to sit on it, because, they are warned, they will catch scabies from it.

In some countries it is common to have presents hanging on, or lying beneath a Christmas Tree. The traditional fir tree, now usually a dead thing lopped off the top of a larger tree and sold for great profit, was introduced into England by Prince Albert shortly after he married Queen Victoria, but the tree itself is just one aspect of the greenery decorations generally associated with Christmas time. Legend says that St Boniface, on his mission from England to Germany in the eighth century, converted Odin's sacred oak into a fir tree decorated in honour of Christ. Whether or not this is true, it shows a popular belief in the antiquity of the Christmas Tree and in its non-Christian origins.

Nina Epton refers to a Spanish custom of bringing in a Christmas Tree:

In Centellas, the boys go out at dawn on Christmas day to cut down the tallest pine they can find in the forests. They bring it back to the village in an ox-cart, take it into the church where they hang it top downwards, on the main altar, and decorate it profusely with fruit and biscuits and there it stays until the day of St Stephen which is a great feast day in Cataluña and prolongs the Christmas festivities. This is the winter solstice counterpart of the summer solstice tree rites observed in so many regions of Spain.

And, we might add, very similar to the bringing in of the May Tree which was once so widespread. Trees, though not necessarily fir trees, were a part of Christmas celebrations in England from an early date, as we can see from an account given in John Stow's *A Survay of London*, first published in 1598, but expanding in subsequent editions in a way similar to Henry Bourne's *Antiquitates Vulgares*:

> Against the Feast of Christmas every man's house, as also their parish churches, were decked with holme, ivy, bayes, and whatsoever the season of the year afforded to be green. The conduits and standards in the streets were likewise garnished: among the which I read that in the year 1444 by tempest of thunder and lightning, towards the morning of Candlemas Day, at the Leadenhall, in Cornhill, a Standard of tree, being set up in the midst of the pavement, fast in the ground, nailed full of holme and ivie, for disport of Christmass to the people, was torne up and cast downe by the malignant Spirit (as was thought,) and the stones of the pavement all about were cast in the streets, and into divers houses, so that the people were sore aghast at the great tempests.

The turning of the year is still a great time for telling tales of the supernatural and Christmas television programmes will invariably include a horror film or a ghost story. A number of customs attached to Midwinter have had their frightening aspects, enhanced by the dark evenings during which many of them took place. Imagine yourself to be a small child in an isolated farmhouse somewhere in the Pennine hills around the border between Yorkshire and Lancashire. On Old Year's Night, you are sitting with the rest of your family by the fire, which is glowing in the iron range, when from outside you hear a faint noise, gradually becoming louder, till it sounds as if a swarm of bees is gathering outside in the darkness. Suddenly the door opens and in steps a group of half-a-dozen or so people, their faces blacked to make them unrecognisable, the men dressed as women, and the women dressed as men with their jackets pulled inside-out. Each carries a broom and, ignoring the members of the household, they sweep around the room, and especially the hearth, humming all the while. When they have finished their cleaning job one of them holds out a purse in which you put a few coppers and they leave for their next call without having said a word. The custom still pops up occasionally in the central Pennine area, in industrial as well as rural areas, though it is nothing like as widespread as it was seventy years ago, when teams of Sweepers or Mummers, both children and adults, came to be looked upon as a nuisance by some people. The custom

Frau Berchta, Alsace.

varied from place to place. Instead of humming, the Sweepers might sing hymns and you could be let off paying them if you broke their solemnity by making them laugh. But the element of disguise was universal—some groups took pride in making themselves unrecognisable—and several people have told me how the Sweepers terrified them when they were young. Reminiscent of the Sweepers, and possibly even more unnerving, are Bavaria's Berchten-Runners. During Advent, these masked figures, whose activities have been revived since World War 2, go around farms demanding small gifts. In Upper Bavaria, they are generally led by women who wield chains, pick-axes and brooms.

Though for many children, and for some adults, Sweeping would have provided an opportunity for licensed begging, the general explanation of its purpose, given by people who used to take part in it, is that the Sweepers were sweeping out the old year to make way for the new, as in some places the back door of a house is opened to let the old year out before the new year is admitted by the front door. It is tempting to see the blackened faces of the sweepers as a mark of luck-bringing, since we often meet with First-Footing customs where the first person to cross the threshold after midnight on New Year's Eve has to have dark hair, carry a lump of coal or have their face smeared with coal-dust; but blackened faces and disguise crop up in all manner of customs all the year round and I am inclined to believe that the element of disguise exists as much as anything to give the wearer the nerve to act in ways which would normally be seen as anti-social or simply embarrassing. The habit of cross-dressing would have a comparable liberating effect, and Henry Bourne, in *Antiquitates Vulgares*, mentions it as a New Year custom which should be condemned:

> There is another Custom observed at this Time, which is called among us *Mumming*; which is a changing of Clothes between Men and Women; who when dress'd in each others Habits, go from one Neighbours' House to another, and partake of their *Christmas Cheer*, and make merry with them in Disguise, by dancing and singing, and such like Merriments. . . .
>
> It were to be wish'd, this Custom, which is still so common among us at this Season of the Year, was laid aside; as it is the Occasion of much Uncleanness and Debauchery, and directly opposite to the Word of GOD.

In some parts of Scotland, the New Year visitors are called Guisers, a name which, like the term 'Mummers', is not confined to any particular place or activity. Children with blackened faces and wearing bizarre clothing go around at Hogmanay (as they do also at Hallowe'en) singing or reciting begging rhymes, and receiving money or food. A correspondent with *The Gentleman's Magazine* referred to this custom back in 1790:

> In Scotland, till very lately (if not in the present time), there was a custom of distributing sweet cakes, and a particular kind of sugared bread, for several days before and after the New Year; and on the last night of the old year (peculiarly called *Hagmenai*) the visitors and company made a point of not separating till after the clock struck twelve, when they rose, and mutually kissing each other, wished each other a happy New Year. Children and others, for several nights, went about from house to house as *Guisarts*, that is, disguised, or in masquerade dresses, singing,
>
> > 'Rise up, good wife, and be no' swier (lazy)
> > To deal your bread as long's you're here;
> > The time will come when you'll be dead,
> > And neither want nor meal nor bread.'
>
> Some of these masquerades had a fiddle, and, when admitted into a house, entertained the company with a dramatic dialogue, partly extempore.

Further south, pre-Christmas visitors might have included Wassailers. In later times they were generally parties of children who went around houses in both rural and urban areas, singing a song which began:

> We've been a while a-wandering among the leaves so green,
> And now we've come a wassailing so plainly to be seen.

Wassailing, Carhampton, Somerset.

After singing they would, of course, beg for gifts and, in Wensleydale, in Yorkshire, they concluded their brief recital by opening a house's letter-box and shouting through the slit, 'Please will you give me my Christmas box!'

In the last century, Wassailers often took a Wassail Bowl or Cup around with them. This was generally a large wooden bowl, decorated and perhaps filled with liquor to be sold to passers-by at exorbitant prices. In *The Gentleman's Magazine* for 1824 there is a description of Christmas customs which includes the following passage:

> The first intimation of Christmas, in Yorkshire, is by what are there called *vessel-cup singers*, generally poor old women, who, about three weeks before Christmas, go from house to house, with a waxen or wooden doll, fantastically dressed, and sometimes adorned with an orange, or a fine rosy-tinged apple. With this in their hands, they sing or chant an old carol, of which the following homely stanza forms a part:
> 'God bless the master of this house,
> The mistress also,
> And all the little children
> That round the table go!'

In the West County, the Wassail Cup was incorporated into the practice of Wassailing cider-apple trees, here described in *The Gentleman's Magazine* of 1791:

In the South-hams of Devonshire, on the eve of Epiphany, the farmer, attended by his workmen, with a large pitcher of cyder, goes to the orchard, and there, encircling one of the best bearing trees, they drink the following toast three several times:

'Here's to thee, old apple-tree,
Whence thou may'st bud, and whence thou may'st blow!
And whence thou may'st bear apples enow!
Hats full! caps full!
Bushel—bushel—sacks full,
And my pockets full too! Huzza!'

This done they return to the house, the doors of which they are sure to find bolted by the females, who, be the weather what it may, are inexorable to all intreaties to open them till someone has guessed at what is on the spit, which is generally some nice little thing, difficult to be hit on, and is the reward of him who first names it. The doors are then thrown open, and the lucky clodpole receives the tit-bit as his recompense. Some are so superstitious as to believe, that if they neglect this custom, the trees will bear no apples that year.

In the recording of apple tree Wassailing mentioned in Chapter 1, the song which the Sealys give is close to the eighteenth-century toast just quoted. For instance they sing:

So well they might bloom, so well they might bear,
That we may have apples and cider this year.

and at the end of the song, the two men shout in chorus:

Hatfuls, capfuls, three bushel bagfuls
Little heap under the stairs,
Hip, hip hooray.

Then Harry Sealy tells how, after the Wassailing, the party would go to the farmer's back door to drink cider and Walter adds:

Oh, they used to fire the gun up in the apple tree to drive the evil spirits out of the tree. And they even used to hang a little bit of toast in the limbs for the robins to come and pick.

In the first chapter I referred to this statement about driving out evil spirits, suggesting that it might have originated with some folkloristic intervention, rather than being the expression of a widespread and ancient folk belief. Even if this is not the case it is wise to approach these evil spirits with some wariness. Are they, perhaps, one old man's rationalisation of the gun-firing—being aware that he is talking about a 'folk' custom—or does he speak of 'evil spirits' in the same way that an engineer might speak of 'gremlins', as the unpredictable problems which can crop up in any human activity, from the cultivation of cider-apple trees to the designing and testing of a new jet engine? To our minds, which we tend to think of as being predominantly rational, the mere mention of supernatural forces like this is enough to trigger off notions of a whole 'primitive' system of belief, shared by the Wassailers, which in turn provides a neat explanation as to why folk customs exist in the first place. But, even with respect to what Walter Sealy says, the evidence for such a system of belief among the Somerset Wassailers is very slender indeed. The firing of guns—and creating a racket generally—is, as we have seen previously and will see again, a feature common to customs in many countries and does not generally have any overt connection with driving off malignant forces.

Certainly the account of Devonshire Wassailing from *The Gentleman's Magazine* contains no such emphasis, merely mentioning that *some* are so superstitious as to believe that neglect of the Wassailing will result in failure of the crop, in the same way that, today, we might say *some* believe they will have bad luck if they walk under a ladder, put new shoes on the kitchen table or look at the new moon through glass. And again, we are dealing with what the writer has been told. We have no way of assessing the depth or limits of the belief. There is no mention in *The Gentleman's Magazine* of the Wassailers firing guns or doing anything to the tree other than toasting it, and at least as much emphasis is given to what happens when the Wassailers return to the house. Here they are Barred-Out (as was the schoolmaster from his school on Shrove Tuesday) and have to play a guessing game to gain entry. Not only does this suggest an essential spirit of fun—rather than any serious ritual upon which the life of the crop really depends—but it also points up the importance of the threshold, real or metaphorical, which is a feature common to many folk customs.

Another instance of Barring-Out occurs in the South Wales Midwinter custom of the Mari Lwyd (generally translated as The Grey Mare, though no one is sure of the name's exact meaning), which still continues in at least one instance, and which was featured in the BBC TV magazine programme 'Nationwide' in late 1978. The Mari Lwyd itself was a skull, generally that of a horse, though sometimes made of wood, fixed on the end of a pole and carried by a bearer who was entirely covered by a sheet. The skull might be decorated with ribbons, have glass eyes etc and it was sometimes buried after use to be dug up the following year. Generally at Christmas, it accompanied a party of men, who went from house to house singing a song which asked for admittance. The people inside had to think up reasons for refusing entrance and, if they ran out of ideas, the party had to be let in and given free ale. 'This would be expensive for a public house', says E. C. Cawte in *Ritual Animal Disguise*, 'where a good improviser might be given free drinks for the evening to keep out the mari lwyd parties'. The party was sometimes accompanied by Punch and Judy, who wore appropriate costumes and had blackened faces, and Punch carried a poker which he beat on the ground as the singing was in progress. Often the party of men with the horse wore their best suits decorated with ribbons, as did some teams of northern England Pace-Eggers, and Judy carried a broom with which she swept around the house inside and out, rather like the New Year's Eve Sweepers we looked at earlier.

The earliest record of the Mari Lwyd comes from around the end of the eighteenth century, but it is only one example of the animal disguises which are generally attached to the Winter months. The only thriving extant example of such disguise in England comes from around north-east Derbyshire, north-west Nottinghamshire and south Yorkshire. During the 1970s, Ian Russell found the Old Tup Play flourishing in villages in this area. The play, which was known of previously but thought to have died out, is generally performed by working-class adolescents, girls as well as boys, who go around local pubs and clubs at Christmas. The characters normally include an Old Man, who introduces the action with a little begging rhyme, and his Wife who fetches a Butcher to kill the Ram they have with them. The Ram, or Tup, disguise comes in many forms, depending on the availability of materials and on the ingenuity and enterprise of the makers, and can range from a wooden head with real horns, mounted on a pole—the bearer wearing a sheepskin coat—to a parka with the hood turned up. The performance, usually brief, ends with the singing of a version of a song widely known as 'The Derby ram', which has been found, without the play, as far away as New Orleans, and describes the immense size of the ram (including, in many versions, its genitals) and the trouble there was in slaughtering it.

Like many other folk customs, the Tup Play has been seen in the past as a pagan survival, in this case of ritual sacrifice, so it is worth bearing in mind Ian Russell's comment that 'the Tup is arguably as active today as it has ever been'. This is understandable when a good evening can raise £10 and a total Christmas' taking can be as much as £150, money which the participants may keep for themselves or use to help out their family's seasonal expenses.

Other examples of similar animal disguise in Midwinter— where the creature consists of a real or manufactured skull or head fixed on a pole, carried by a bearer who is generally crouched, hidden by a sheet, blanket or similar covering—are given by E. C. Cawte. The Hooden Horse in Kent usually came out on Christmas Eve. It took the form of a wooden decorated head, with a moveable jaw, and was accompanied by a small party of men on its journey round the houses. After a song (which in some cases resembled the one used for Wassailing apple trees) the party would be admitted. One of them, the Mollie, dressed as a woman, swept the floor and pursued the girls around the room and, after general foolery, the men were given money and moved on to the next house.

In a similar area to the Old Tup was the Old Horse (it should be borne in mind that, in this part of England, 'old' is as much a term of familiarity or affection as it is an indicator of actual age). The Old Horse was a real skull or wooden head with a moveable jaw, fixed on a pole and carried by a man who was covered with a sheet. The group sang a song detailing the Old Horse's decline (in this case he really was old) while a blacksmith mimed the shoeing of the recalcitrant beast. A collection was taken.

E. C. Cawte mentions a horse from southern Austria, which was accompanied by two smiths who tried to shoe him, and, in fact, there are numerous examples of animal disguise all over Europe, many of them with distinct resemblances to comparable English customs. One of the earliest references in Christian times comes from the fourth century, when the Bishop of Barcelona reproached himself for having encouraged a Stag Play, by a condemnatory description, giving details of the play itself and of the costume worn in it. St Augustine inveighed against people dressing up like a horse or a stag and, from thirteenth-century France, in the diocese of Elne, near Perpignan, comes an account of how boys used to ride in church on or in a wooden horse, though they had been forbidden to do so. Punishment came when one rider, with his horse, was consumed by flames. In later times, increasing with the growing interest in folklore, there are instances of cows, bulls, horses, stags, goats, bears—often unruly and sometimes bawdy creatures—being led around, assaulted, slaughtered, shaken to pieces, accompanied by various differing characters,

Hobby Horse and Assistants,
Stuttgart, Germany.

often including a man dressed as a woman.

In an area around the mouth of the River Trent in north Lincolnshire, a horse sometimes accompanied the Wooing Play, between Christmas and Plough Monday. It was of a different type from the English horses described above, being made from a farm sieve slung from the bearer's shoulders, which were covered with a cloth. At the front end of the sieve was fastened a head—generally made of wood—though on odd occasions constructed from an old plough—and at the rear was a tail which often had hooks or tin tacks in it. Of all the Winter animals, this horse is the only one which bears any resemblance to what we normally think of as a Hobby Horse, a framework fastened to the waist or chest of the bearer, whose arms are free and who pretends to be actually riding the horse. References to this kind of horse appear frequently from the end of the sixteenth century to the first quarter of the seventeenth, during which period it was connected with civic pageants, guild processions and so on, and was often associated with the Morris Dancers who appeared on such occasions. But this horse seems to have virtually died out by the middle of the seventeenth century—to await folkloristic revival in the nineteenth century—and the more primitive constructions are apparently a much later phenomenon. E. C. Cawte has this to say about them:

> The hooded animals recorded since 1800 have enough in common to regard them as one class. There is evidence neither for a hooded animal much before that date, nor for an association between the hooded animal and the morris dance, nor that this type of construction was ever called a hobby-horse before this

*Wren Bush and Wren Boys,
1850 engraving.*

century. The common though not invariable features of the hooded animals are the construction, the Christmas performance, the begging song (or spoken appeal in some places), and the accompanying performers, especially the shemale; Mollie with her broom in Kent, Judy with her broom in Wales, and Our Old Lass with the Old Tup (though rarely with a broom).

If these animals are of such recent origin, what were the influences that caused them to come into being and what functions did they perform during their comparatively brief existences? Such questions remain to be answered and will probably never be decided conclusively,

There is another custom which was occasionally accompanied by a Hobby Horse, that of Hunting the Wren. According to Colonel Vallancey, writing of Ireland in the eighteenth century, the wren:

> ... *is still hunted and killed by the peasants on Christmas Day,* and on the following (St. Stephen's Day) he is carried about hung by the leg in the centre of two hoops crossing each other at right angles, and a procession made in every village, of men, women, and children, singing an Irish catch, importing him to be the king of all birds.

The practice still goes on in some parts of Ireland, kept up by young boys, who sometimes black their faces or dress as girls.

They do not generally have a wren, but still have a begging 'catch', which Seán Ó Suilleabháin gives as:

> The wren, the wren, the king of all birds,
> St. Stephen's Day was caught in the furze;
> Although he is little, his family is great,
> So rise up, landlady, and give us a treat;
> Bottles of whiskey and bottles of beer,
> And I wish you all a happy New Year.

In addition to Ireland, the custom has been recorded in Wales and, in the Isle of Man, it heralded the arrival of Christmas. It was also known in France and an eighteenth-century traveller tells of the form it took at Le Ciotat, near Marseilles, towards the end of December:

> . . . a numerous body of men, armed with swords and pistols, set off in search of a very small bird which the ancients call Troglodytes. . . . When they have found it (a thing not difficult, because they always take care to have one ready), it is suspended on the middle of a pole, which two men carry on their shoulders, as if it were a heavy burthen. This whimsical procession parades round the town; the bird is weighed in a great pair of scales, and the company then sits down to table and makes merry.

The ironic tone affected by the writer seems not only to reflect his own irreverent attitude towards these goings-on but also the demeanour of the people who took part in the custom in what was apparently an extremely light-hearted way.

In England, especially in the north and Midlands, there was foolery on Plough Monday, the Monday after Twelfth Day, which was traditionally supposed to be the date when the year's ploughing began. In fact the day tended to be given over to feasting and recreation. Writing under the pseudonym of T. Row, the Derbyshire antiquary, Samuel Pegge, described what went on, in the pages of *The Gentleman's Magazine* for 1762:

> . . . *Plough-Monday* . . . is when the labour of the Plough and other rustic toils begin. On this day the young men yoke themselves and *draw* a PLOUGH *about* with Musick, and one or two persons, in antic dresses, like Jack-Puddings, go from house to house, to gather money to drink. If you refuse them, they plough up your dunghill. We call them here the Plough Bullocks.

And John Brand, in the 1777 edition of '*Popular Antiquities*', talks about what are presumably his own experiences of Plough Monday in north-east England (noting that similar customs used to be observed at Lent):

RIGHT
*Plough Monday, Barling,
Cambridgeshire, 1952.*

BELOW
*Sword Dance, Goathland Plough
Stots, North Yorkshire.*

The *Fool Plough* goes about, a Pageant that consists of a Number of *Sword Dancers*, dragging a Plough, with Music, and one, sometimes two, in a very antic Dress; the *Bessy*, in the grotesque Habit of an *old Woman*, and the *Fool*, almost covered with Skins, a hairy Cap on, and the Tail of some Animal hanging from his Back: The Office of one of these *Characters* is, to go rattling a Box amongst the Spectators of the Dance, in which he collects their little Donations.

Both Brand and Pegge acknowledge that one of the motives for staging the customs was to get money (and the Plough Bullocks, who probably imbibed as they went on their travels, took speedy revenge on the stingy).

Gain was also one of the motives for my paternal grandparents when, as children some eighty years ago, they too went around on Plough Monday through the streets of Long Eaton, a small town in east Derbyshire. They had no plough, but they did black their faces and turn their jackets inside out, and they carried brooms (though not to sweep with). Sometimes the boys would wear their mother's jackets. They went around the houses singing:

Plough Monday, Shrove Tuesday when the boys went to plough,
My mother made some pancakes and she didn't know how.
She buttered them, she sugared them, she made them turn black,
She put some rat poison in to poison poor Jack.

'After we'd been singing one or two songs, you see, we used to sing that', said my grandmother, 'and then we knocked at the door and of course the people came to the door. When they saw you they asked you in the house and sometimes they'd give you something to eat or they'd give you ha'pennies and pennies. And of course we'd got a chip shop in the district and we used to go and buy chips and eat them'.

Further on in his account of Plough Monday activities quoted above, John Brand states his belief that the characters of the Fool and Bessy 'are plainly Fragments of the antient *Festival of Fools*, held on New Year's Day'. The Festival of Fools was widespread throughout mediaeval times up to the Reformation and beyond, though Puritan thought condemned it roundly. It was not just confined to New Year's Day; it seems that, for instance, at one time in London, it commenced on Hallowe'en and continued until the Monday after 26 December. The custom centred round the election, within a particular group, of a figure of authority who would preside over the festivities, often unruly, for an allotted term. In England, this figure was generally the Lord of

Plough Monday: Bessy and the Fool. A fanciful representation, c.1850.

Misrule and, in Scotland, the Abbott of Unreason. France had its *Abbés de Malgouvré* and *de Liesse*, and both Scotland and France had Boy Bishops. These turn-of-the-year revels were enjoyed by both high and low, clergy and laity. Lords of Misrule and Masters of Revels could be found in university colleges and civic households, among Lords on their estates and in the Inner Temple, and it is recorded that a certain George Ferrers was Lord of Misrule for the twelve days of Christmas when Edward VI kept open house at Greenwich in 1553. Phillip Stubbes, whose disapproving description of May customs was quoted earlier on, also had harsh words for the Lords of Misrule:

> Firste, all the wilde heades of the parishe, conventynge together, chuse them a grand Capitaine (of mischeef) whom they innoble with the title of my *Lorde of Misserule*, and hym they crown with great solemnitie, and adopte for their kyng. This kyng anoynted, chuseth for the twentie, fourtie, three score, or a hundred lustie guttes like to hymself, to wait uppon his lordely majestie, and to guarde his noble persone. Then every one of these his menne he investeth with his liveries, of greene, yellowe, or some other light wanton colour. And as though that were not (baudie) gaudy enough I should saie, they bedecke themselves with scarfes, ribons, and laces, hanged all over with golde rynges, precious stones, and other jewelles: this doen, they tye about either legge twentie or fourtie belles with rich hande-kercheefes, in their hands, and sometymes laied acrosse over their shoulders and neckes, borrowed for the moste part of their pretie Mopsies and loovyng Bessies for bussyng them in the darcke. Thus thinges

sette in order, they have their Hobbie horses, Dragons, and other antiques, together with their baudie Pipers, and thunderyng Drommers, to strike up the Deville's Daunce withall, then marche these Heathen companie towards the Church and Churche-yard, their Pipers pipyng, Drommers thonderying, their stumppes dauncyng, their Belles iynglyng, their handkerchefes swyngyng about their heades like madmen, their Hobbie horses, and other Monsters skyrmishyng amongest the throng: and in this sorte they goe to the Churche, (though the Minister bee at Praier or Preachyng) dauncyng and swingyng their handkercheefes over their heades, in the Churche, like Devilles incarnate, with suche a confused noise, that no man can heare his owne voice.

After the revellers have sufficiently gained the attention of the congregation, who go so far as to stand on the pews to see better, they go back out into the churchyard:

> . . . where they have commonly their sommer haules, their Bowers, Arbours, and Banquettyng Houses set up, wherein they feaste, banquet, and daunce all that daie, and (peradventure) all that night too. And thus these terrestrial furies spend their Sabbaoth daie.

Stubbes then continues his vivid account by saying that the company gives Lord of Misrule badges, made of paper, to anyone who gives money to support the festivities, rather as people collecting for charities do today. Supplies of provisions are also made:

> An other sorte of fantasticall fooles bring to these Hellhoundes (the Lord of Misrule and his complices) some Bread, some good Ale, some newe Cheese, some olde Cheese, some Custardes, some Cakes, some Flaunes, some Tartes, some Creame, some Meate, some one thing, some another: but if they knewe that as often as they bring any to the maintainance of these execrable pastymes, they offer sacrifice to the Devill and Sathanas, they would repent, and withdrawe their handes, which God graunt they maie.

While Stubbes' anger at the invasion of the church is under-standable enough (though in earlier times churches and church-yards were often used for secular enjoyment as well as religious worship) it does seem that his main objection is to people enjoy-ing themselves. However, in Amiens, in the twelfth century, the election of a Boy Bishop to preside over the Feast of Fools did lead to apparently open mockery of the Church, including a mock mass, dancing and obscene songs, food eaten from the altar and games of cards and dice played there as well. But this does not necessarily imply anti-Christian spirit, since the revellers were themselves of the ecclesiastical fraternity, so perhaps it was another example of the Church's periodic willingness to embrace, or at least tolerate, practices which had a decidedly non-Christian air. At times, however, the more high-minded members of the clergy did feel that things had gone too far. For instance, in 1265, Archbishop Odo of Sens managed to suppress the more obscene elements of the Feast of Fools, while allowing the celebrations themselves to continue. Though widespread and popular throughout Europe, the Feast did not generally survive the Reformation (although there is a record that it still existed in 1645 in the monastery of the Cordeliers at Antibes) but I think it reasonable to suggest that the spirits of the Lord of Misrule and his band are still with us around the time of Christmas and the New Year, in the excesses of celebration generally and, more specifically, at the Christmas office party where, traditionally, rigid codes of behaviour and etiquette which apply for the rest of the year are broken down, and where the office 'wag' is allowed to take liberties that would normally result in his dismissal. It is even possible to hire a professional organiser of games and merriment for office parties and similar functions, just as a Lord of Misrule could be hired in the past.

4. Dance and drama

O
N BOXING DAY MORNING of 1899, Cecil Sharp looked out of the window of a friend's house in Headington Quarry near Oxford, where he, with his family, was spending Christmas. A group of men walked up the drive and performed a strange dance before the house to the accompaniment of a concertina. Sharp was enthralled and, after the dancing had finished, he quizzed the men enthusiastically and noted down five of their tunes. He discovered that they were the local Morris team, or 'side', who normally danced at Whitsuntide, but were out in Midwinter because Christmas funds were low. This was Sharp's earliest first-hand encounter with the dances, and the music, that he came to champion, till in time he became this century's most hard-working and passionate collector and disseminator of folk dance and song. He was already in early middle age, plagued by asthma, but he devoted the rest of his days, until his death in 1924, to giving back to the English people, through books and public demonstration, the traditional music and dances which had been so much in decline during the previous century.

Sharp was not the first to have recognised the value of this apparently rich legacy. In 1898, a Folk Song Society had been formed in an attempt to unify the work of the collectors who had been going busily round the country noting down songs from the working people there, and the existence of Morris Dancing was also well known. But in the case of the dance it was Sharp who, with his friend Herbert MacIlwaine, had set out methodically to collect and publish information, so that it would be available to a wider public. It is largely as a result of their work that we are able to witness the performances of groups like the Morris men who began this book, not only on the village green or in the town square, but in folk music festivals and in any film or television drama, documentary or news programme that needs a little bit of 'local colour'. We tend to think of Morris Dancers as a Spring phenomenon—with little bells strapped to their shins and

*Headington Morris, Oxfordshire,
early 1900s.*

wearing flower-bedecked hats—but this impression is based upon
the Cotswold Morris, like Headington Quarry for instance, which
did appear mainly at Whitsuntide, whereas comparable dances
were once performed in other areas and at other times of the
year: in north-west England, for instance, during Wakes Week
in late Summer, at the time of the annual Rushcart processions,
which went through the streets carrying the rushes which were
to be strewn on the floors of the local churches; at Christmas in
the counties bordering Wales, and also between Christmas and
Plough Monday in East Anglia, when the Mollie Dancers came
out; and there were also the Midwinter Sword Dances in Yorkshire and in north-east England. These dances are usually
grouped together as 'ceremonial', because of the elements they
have in common, being performed at fairly specific times of the
year by bands of men (though a female-dominated Carnival
Morris has sprung up in the north-west in this century), dressed
in special costume for the occasion, and operating as integrated
groups dancing more or less elaborate steps to trace ground
patterns which, in the case of Sword Dancers can result in the
weaving of the swords into a star-shaped pattern. The exuberant

*Handsworth Sword Dancers,
Yorkshire, c.1912.*

leaping of the Whitsuntide dancers and their time of appearance
has led to suggestions that they represent the decayed remnants
of magical fertility ceremonies and the fact that Sword Dances
have concluded with the mock execution of an ancillary member
of the team has suggested to some writers the possibility that the
dance is the relic of what was once real human sacrifice. Ideas
such as these are seductively romantic, but would be extremely
difficult, if not impossible, to prove. If the dances ever did function
in such ways in England, there is no record of the fact and it is
foolish to entertain the notion that they would have survived
quite vigorously with no impetus other than habit for many centuries until their virtual demise during the nineteenth century.
We also tend to be misled by the notion that these dances are
specifically English in character and that they have always been
confined to isolated rural places, where, as everyone knows,
strange goings-on tend to occur. In fact, similar dances have
been known and are known all over Europe and our notion of
their scarcity is more the result of the limitations of past research
than a reflection of reality. We can only speculate on the origins
of the Morris Dance ('Morris' is one of those all-purpose words
like 'Mummer' and 'Guiser' and has also been used to denote
customs which do not include dancing) but it is certain that,
during the sixteenth century, a form or forms of the dance became
so popular as to be chic. No civic occasion or guild procession
was complete without its team of Morris men and, in 1583,
would-be colonists setting sail from Plymouth to Newfoundland
took Morris Dancers with them for their own entertainment and

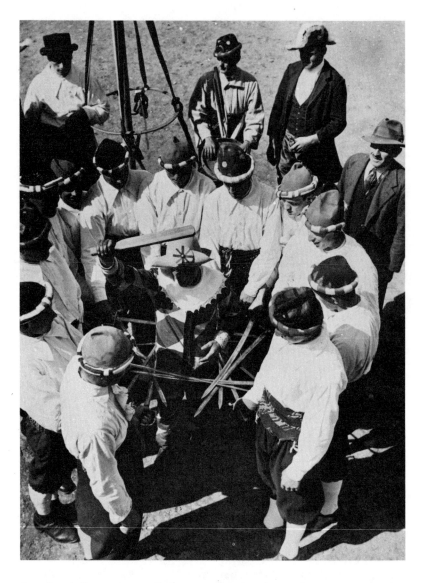

Fenestrelle Sword Dance, Italy.

for the 'allurement of the Savages'. They also appeared for
diversion in stage plays of this period and featured prominently
in the popular May Games, along with Robin Hood and his band
who, again, were fashionable figures. On such occasions, the
dancers were often accompanied by a tourney-type Hobby
Horse, a Fool carrying a wooden collecting label and a Maid
Marian. The latter was sometimes a woman, but more often a
boy or man dressed in female clothing, that ubiquitous character
who, in later times, also appeared with the East Anglian, Derbyshire and north-west Morris, and with the Sword Dancers too.

With the Reformation, the Morris lost much of its tremendous
popularity. It parted company with the Hobby Horse and went

*Morris Dancers and their
Attendants. 19th? century
drawing based on early 16th-
century painted glass window.*

underground. From what we can piece together of these early
dances, they seem to have resembled the familiar Cotswold type
which survived into the last century. The men generally wore
bells, had white shirts decorated with ribbons or crossed bald-
ricks, carried handkerchiefs and danced to the music of the pipe
and tabor. Although the later Cotswold teams of six men and a
Fool are generally associated with Whitsuntide, they also
appeared for the May celebrations and were quite accustomed
to use their skill to earn money at other times of the year. Some
teams would dance a circuit to London and back to raise funds
during the Summer months. Nor were they the effeminate
creatures folk dancers are popularly supposed to be. The dancing
is a strenuous business, and I have seen a group of mainly middle-
aged men at Bampton-in-the-Bush in Oxfordshire keep up a pace
which would have exhausted many younger men.

Some revival teams have been accused of 'giving the Morris

*Morris Dancers, Chipping
Camden, Oxfordshire, c.1900.*

a bad name' by their excessive drinking, but this seems to be an old tradition, perhaps as old as the Morris itself, which in the past has led to some disarray. At the end of the last century, for instance, the Bampton men were accustomed to dance their way into the village from the outskirts, stopping at houses on the way to drink home brew. Often they became so drunk that they lost step and bumped into each other, after which fighting would start and the team would disband. Similarly, in the north-west of England, the Morris Dancers were generally considered to be the most unruly element of the Wakes festivities, notorious for their drunkenness and brawling. Such instances suggest that enjoyment was an important part of the Morris men's activities and puts their dancing in a context other than the pure mechanics of the dances themselves, or of ideas of pre-Christian ritual, which are imposed by the folklorist who observes only what he or she wants to observe and then uses these selective observations to suggest motives which may not have been in the minds of the dancers at all.

The question of motives becomes even more complex and bewildering when we realise that English ceremonial dances have impressively strong parallels throughout Europe and even further afield. There are many dances from Spain (see 'Ritual dances' by Lucile Armstrong in *Folk Music Journal* 1978), and

Lancashire Morris Side from the Oldham area, possibly Royton, c.1910.

Knutsford Morris, Cheshire. May Day, c.1900.

also from France, Italy, Greece, Romania and Bali, which have features in common with English dances. The multicoloured jackets decorated with ribbons and worn by Castilian Stilt Dancers are very similar to those worn by some English Morris Dancers and, moreover, the figures in the Castilian dances bear a marked resemblance to those of the English Morris Dance. The Spanish Basques of Guipuzcoa and the Bacup Coconut Dancers of north-west England perform similar garland dances, in which each dancer carries an arch decorated with coloured paper or a tuft of ribbons. Widespread also are the stick dances, which are executed in a manner similar to that of the Cotswold dancers. There are Sword Dances too, involving figures similar to those of the north-east English dances, where the dancers form a con-

Stilt Dancers, Aquitaine, France.

La Soule Hobby Horse and troupe, 1948.

*Basque Garland Dancers,
Bayonne, France, 1927.*

*Brittania Coconut Dancers,
Bacup, Lancashire.*

97

Portuguese Stick Dancers.

tinuous chain by holding onto the tips of their partner's swords; John Brand was struck by the similarity between Sword Dances he had seen in Northumberland and an account of a Swedish Sword Dance written by the ecclesiast Olaus Magnus and published in Rome in 1555.

But what is the significance of such similarities between dances over such a wide area? To produce even a tentative answer would involve immense scholarly labour and would also mean working at first hand for long periods with individual groups of dancers throughout Europe at least, and being familiar not only with their respective languages but also with their means of earning a living, their social status and the relationships within each group, the social, political and economic histories of each region and country and so forth.

It is all very well to suggest, for example, that the sticks used in a dance from Burgos in Spain represent the planting sticks of ancient man, that dancing in a figure of eight represents continuity of time or infinity, or that the human 'horse', whose shoeing is mimed in the dance is symbolic of fertility; there remains the problem of invoking symbols which can signify a

multitude of different things, depending on who you are and where and when you live. The horse can be a symbol of fertility (or of sexual potency) but it can also be a symbol of economic strength, of warlike capacity, of freedom, or of fooling around (as in 'horseplay' or 'horsing about'), very much in the unruly way that many of the Hobby Horses we looked at earlier have conducted themselves. What we really need to know is what the dancers themselves, and the community around them, thought of what they were doing. Thus we learn that the Romanian

Arexenaga Sword Dancers, Oldarra.

RIGHT
Baile *of hoops, Villafranca, Spain.*

BELOW
Romanian Caluşari performing a
ceremonial healing dance,
London, 1935.

Goathland Mummers, North Yorkshire, c.1900.

Caluşari, when visiting England in 1935, danced on the train all the way across Europe because 'If we don't dance our crops will not grow' and, in English Morris dancing, the striking of sticks on the ground is said to 'waken the earth spirits'. The significance of such statements, which in any case are few and far between, is impossible to assess, made, as they would be, to people 'in the know' and perhaps as the result of a certain amount of unconscious prompting.

Similar problems arise when we come to the subject of the folk play. At certain times of the year, often at Christmas, but also around All Souls, New Year, Plough Monday and Easter according to location, within living memory, groups of men or boys would be out in the streets, dressed sometimes in elaborate costume, sometimes with the simplest props, performing the little dramas which have caused so much speculation among folklorists. These Mummers, Guisers, Pace-Eggers, Plough Jags etc were not 'trained' actors (though they would often be coached by older relatives), but could be called semi-professional since a collection was invariably taken. They were also peripatetic, performing out in the open, or in private houses, pubs, clubs and suchlike places, and they acted in a variety of styles from the humorous to the declamatory, often combining different styles in one performance. The type of play varied according to broad location and the most common form, which folklorists call the 'Hero-Combat', was widespread throughout north, central and southern England, the south of Scotland and Northern Ireland. The central dramatic theme of the Hero-Combat Plays revolves around the killing of one or more adversaries by a self-proclaimed warrior and their subsequent revival by a comic doctor. The hero might be Alexander, St George, King George etc, and adversaries included the King of Egypt, the Black Moroccan Prince, Bold Slasher and the Indian King. The recurring theme of death and revival has led many people, including myself, to see the plays as

Chithurst Tipteers, Sussex,
Christmas 1900.

debased fertility rites of non-Christian or pre-Christian origin. So, for instance, in *The Mummers' Play*, published posthumously after his death in World War 1, Reginald Tiddy maintains that:

> [the play] now possesses hardly any of the qualities that we look for in a drama. There is no hint of a continuous chain of events leading up to and down from a crisis: there is no suggestion of the interplay of character and circumstance. Yet the Mummers' Play, degenerate and undeveloped though it may be, bears distinct traces of a ritual origin. . . .

The idea that the differing varieties of folk play are degenerate forms of a single original—probably close to recorded Balkan examples where the motifs of fertility, including overt sexual foolery, are prominent—is still with us, but begins to seem more and more like speculative fantasy. There is, for instance, no evidence for the existence of this type of play in England before the early eighteenth century and most records come from the nineteenth and twentieth centuries. In the north of England, from around the mid-1740s to as late as the 1950s, texts of the plays were printed in little pamphlets called 'chapbooks', and run off in large editions, so it is fair to assume that, whatever the plays' origins, there was increasing interest in them during this period. They were not just being passed down by word of mouth, but could be learned by interested groups directly from print.

In his essay 'Popular drama and the mummers' play', A. E. Green maintains that, since 'even eighteenth-century references are rare, and do not occur where we might expect to find them',

Symondsbury Mummers, Dorset, 1952.

Overton Mummers, Hampshire, c.1930.

it is 'a fair inference . . . that the growth in the number of refer-ences during the nineteenth century broadly reflects a growth in the number of local plays (albeit variants of a small number of main types) . . . even when rural in provenance, these plays are the property, and their performance is the expression, of an agrarian proletariat, not a peasantry; and their provenance is just as often the small town or the industrial village'.

The widespread existence of the chapbooks has resulted in a certain standardisation of versions of plays collected orally from the north of England, but the pamphlets were probably seen as guides to performance rather than as inviolable texts. Here are the words of the Pace-Egg Play as it was performed on Good Friday around the village of Blackshaw Head in the West York-shire Pennines, near the border with Lancashire, shortly before World War 1. While it closely resembles chapbook texts, it is considerably shorter than the printed versions:

ALL
> A ring, a ring, we enter in
> To see this merry act begin.
> We'll act it right, we'll act it left,
> We'll act it on a public scale,
> And if you don't believe these words I say
> Step in St George, and clear my way.

ST GEORGE
> I am St George, the noble bright,
> Who shed his blood for England's right
> —England's right, England's left—
> I'll make thee cry thy blood away.

SLASHER
> How canst thou make me cry my blood
> away
> Since my head is made of steel,
> My body made of brass,
> My hands and feet of knuckle-bone?
> I challenge thee to fight.

Cross swords

> Pardon, grant and fight.

ST GEORGE
> What now, bold Slasher's dead and gone,
> What must become of me?
> He challenged me to fight,
> Why should I deny it?
> I struck his body in ten parts
> And sent him o'er the sea to make mince
> pies.
> Mince pies hot, mince pies cold,

Mince pies in a dish, eight or nine (nine or
ten) days old.
If there be a Doctor in this world
We'll have one if it costs ten thousand
pounds,
Doctor, doctor.

DOCTOR   In comes I who never came yet,
With my great head and little wit.
Although my wit it is but small
Perhaps I've enough to serve you all.

ST GEORGE   Are you the Doctor?

DOCTOR   Yes sir, I'm the Doctor.

ST GEORGE   How came you to be the Doctor?

DOCTOR   By my travels, sir.

ST GEORGE   How far have you travelled?

DOCTOR   From Italy, Octley (sic), Germany, France
and Spain,
And now returned to cure diseases in old
England again.

SLASHER   Oh my back.

DOCTOR   What's the miss with thy back?

SLASHER   My back is broken, my heart confounded,
The like I've never known it before.

DOCTOR   I have a bottle to cure any complaint.
Take a little of this bottle
And let it run down thy throttle.
If thou be not quite slain
Rise up, bold Jack, and fight thy round over
again.

SLASHER   Oh my back.

DOCTOR   Oh, I forgot. I have in my bag
A bottle called Death to any complaint.
Take a little of this bottle.
I have in my bag plasters for broken-backed
mice,
Pack-saddles and panniards for grasshoppers.

BLACK MORROCCO PRINCE	I am the Black Morrocco Prince. Through the hills and through the dales I make my bells to ring. I am he who came to fight For the King of Egypt's daughter, And brought the fiery dragon to the slaughter.

Fight

ST GEORGE	Poor old soldier, dead and gone. What must become of me? He challenged me to fight, Why should I deny it?
ALL [*singing*]	Ho the next that steps up is th'old Tosspot you see, He's a gallant old man and he wears a pig-tail.
TOSSPOT [*singing*]	I've some eggs in my basket although I appear Exaspecting (eggaspecting) Summer time coming in for my share. (When the hens start to lay again.) Although I am ragged and not so well dressed I can carry some Pace Eggs as well as the best. I've a stick in my hand and a pipe in my snout, And an old tally-wife who is better than bout.
ALL [*singing*]	We're a ring of fine lads as ever you saw (you've seen), We can all sing as merry as Robin in glin (i' t' dean). Come search up your Pace Eggs and see we do right To treat our bonny lasses at Todmorden Fair. Come search up your Pace Eggs and see we do right, If you give us nowt we'll take nowt, farewell and goodbye (neet).

This is a typical play of the Hero-Combat variety, remembered by the late Mr Harry Greenwood, who took part in it when he was a boy of about twelve years old, and published in *Memories* in 1976.

> Two months or more before Good Friday, boys who were to be in the play (no girls were included) [though a revival after the War did include one girl] would meet at each other's homes around Blackshaw, and their mothers would 'tutor' them in the words and actions—'they knew it off by heart did mothers'. The week before Good Friday they would sew ribbons on the boys' Sunday suits, 'red, white and blue, and all sorts . . . and we were all decked up wi' ribbons'.
>
> On Good Friday the boys performed the play at surrounding houses and farms. . . . They collected about five shillings each, [a substantial amount] 'and then went off to Todmorden Fair at night' walking both ways.
>
> The play was handed down orally ('it wasn't written down, you all knew it'), and the participants seemed to have changed quite rapidly:
>
> Me eldest brother went for a start—and then I would go, you know. Then me younger brother would take hold. Went through the family like that, you see.

A universal feature of the folk plays is the appearance (often brief) of characters who contribute nothing to the main action. In the above play such a character was Tosspot, who had a blackened face and wore one black clog and one white clog. In some instances (for the play was widely performed in the area, sometimes with a number of bands covering the same territory, vying for attention and money) Tosspot wore a pig-tail on his back, made from plainted straw with pins stuck in it. In one hand he carried a basket of eggs and in the other his tally-wife (common-law wife), Our Mary Anne, who was a straw doll. It seems to have been Tosspot who took the inevitable collection and he also had more license than the other characters, for he was allowed to improvise his lines for humorous effect and, like the Wild Horse with the Cheshire Souling play (also a character unrelated to the action), he caused havoc among the spectators, chasing girls and making a general nuisance of himself.

Whatever the origins of the Pace-Egg Play, and they will almost certainly remain obscure, Mr Greenwood accepted it as part of the yearly round—'I don't know how it started . . . we were just brought up to it'. There are certainly a number of reasons why the play at that time should be seen as a thriving concern, rather than as a primitive survival. First, it provided recreation, not just on Good Friday but in the previous months of rehearsal; something to do at a time before the existence of radio and

Fanciful engraving of Wild Man or Woodhouse, a common figure in 16th-century pageants, c.1810.

television when, as many old people will tell you, 'You had to make your own entertainment'. Secondly it provided a sense of social continuity and cohesion, since most of the male members of the community would have taken part in the play at one time or another, and the mothers played their part in the 'tutoring' and making the costumes. Thirdly, perhaps most importantly for the boys, the play provided a source of income in a community which, while not poor, was nevertheless not generally affluent. These are the kind of mundane rationalisations that can only be arrived at by knowing something about the people who take part in a custom and the place that custom has in the life of a community; the kind of information that, until recently, has not much interested folklorists, who have been keener to speculate about origins and to point out the striking international parallels in folk drama and other customs. Of course such parallels do exist—they are one of the great dilemmas of folklore. Frazer, for instance, refers to the Whitsuntide custom in Saxony and Thüringen of:

> 'chasing the Wild Man out of the bush,' or 'fetching the Wild Man out of the Wood.' A young fellow is enveloped in leaves or moss and called the Wild Man. He hides in the wood and the other lads of the village go out to seek him. They find him, lead him captive out of the wood, and fire at him with blank muskets. He falls like dead to the ground, but a lad dressed as a doctor bleeds him, and he comes to life again. At this they rejoice, and, binding him fast on a waggon, take him to the village, where they tell all the people how they have caught the Wild Man. At every house they receive a gift.

Then there are the plays from Macedonia and Thessaly, re-ported in the early years of this century—involving a marriage, the death of the bridegroom, his lamentation by the bride and subsequent revival—which have been likened to the east Mid-lands Wooing Plays.

Rodney Gallop saw a play in a village near Torres Vedras in Portugal on Carnival Sunday in 1932, where the Mummers set up a screen in the open near the church and, one by one, emerged from behind it:

> The first to appear wore a battered top hat and frayed frock coat and carried a black bag in his hand. Singing his lines unaccom-panied he announced that he was a doctor, famous throughout Europe and able to cure any disease. Two more characters now entered, a peasant and his wife. The first wore an old-fashioned broad felt hat and side-whiskers, and carried a striped saddle-

12 *Brittania Coconut Dancers, Bacup, Lancashire.*

LEFT
13 *Chairing of the Mayor of Ock Street, Abingdon, Oxfordshire.*

FAR LEFT
*14 Headington Morris,
Oxfordshire.*

LEFT
*15 Grenoside Rapper Sword
Dancers, Yorkshire, with swords
formed into a 'knut'.*

BELOW
*16 Yorkshire Chandelier Clog
Dancing Team.*

FAR LEFT
17 Midgley Pace-Eggers, Yorkshire, performing their traditional play.

LEFT
18 Ripon Sword Dancers' Play, Yorkshire.

BELOW
19 Haxey Hood Game: the Fool's Speech, Haxey, Lincolnshire.

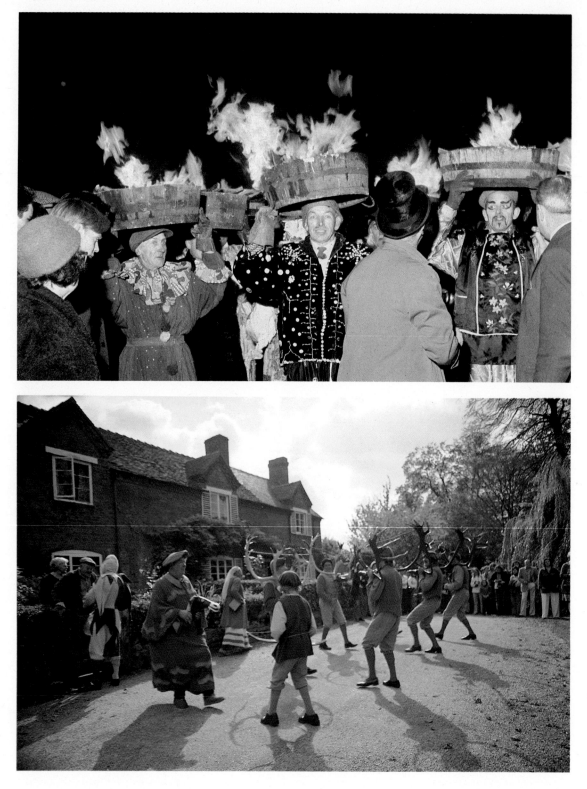

20 *Guysers carrying blazing tar barrels, Fire Ceremony, Allendale, Northumberland.*

22 *Shrovetide horse-racing, Denmark.*

23 *Early Valentine Card.*

21 *Horn Dancers and attendants, Abbotts' Bromley, Staffordshire.*

cloth over his shoulder. His lady, in check dress and cunningly devised 'kerchief and veil, acted her part so well that our suspicions of her real sex were not confirmed until a pleasant tenor voice betrayed her.

The dialogue which followed, and indeed the whole play, was sung in quatrains to the same tune. The wife described her symptoms at great length, and the husband eloquently implored the doctor's aid. Presently there entered a new character wearing a white overall and bringing a chair on which the lady sat down with heart-rending groans to be examined by the doctor.... A moment later, with a deft gesture, the doctor slipped his hand under the chair and whipped out—a celluloid doll.

For Gallop, the play exemplified the 'magic birth of ancient ritual', an act of sympathetic magic whereby 'the fertility of the village and all that went to its sustenance had been assured for the coming year'. However, he goes on to admit that the actors 'were not consciously aware of this. They had in fact written the lines of their play themselves that very year. But their theme had been determined by an ancient tradition, its roots lost in the mists of the past'. The questions raised by such a commentary are mostly unanswerable. If the actors in such plays are unaware of the true 'significance' of what they are doing, was there ever a time when they were aware? Are magical motives a major driving force in the actors' unconscious minds or are they exotic fantasies conjured up as part of the observer's response? To use evocative phrases like 'the mists of the past' is just further mystification to cover up the folklorist's ignorance of origins.

Unfortunately Rodney Gallop does not give any of the reasons the actors themselves may have advanced for performing the play, nor does he say what model they used, whether they were sticking closely to an established traditional plot or believed that they were creating something which was essentially new. In the end we are left with the bare bones of the play, as the folklorist observed it, as is the case with most descriptions of these dramas which appear so strange and symbol-laden to the outsider, but which were plainly common currency to the people who took part in them and to the communities in which they were acted out. To understand the real significance of the plays we need to know what their meaning is to the participants (both players and spectators, the division is not necessarily distinct) and this is information which, in most cases, we simply do not possess.

5. *The human seasons*

SO FAR WE HAVE LOOKED at the kind of customs in which people have taken part at various times of the year, and which appear to cluster around either times of seasonal change or significance, or times of agricultural importance. Some customs, like those of Spring and harvest seem directly linked in form and/or content to the times at which they appear, while others, for instance the appearance of humans masquerading as animals around Midwinter, seem to have no relevance to their particular season. At least it may be said that, however we interpret them, many of these customs represent some kind of response from a community to particular 'thresholds' of the year and, even if only a small group within the community is directly involved in the staging of the custom, the community as a whole is expected to show its compliance and approval by bestowing gifts of food, drink or money on the group. In this chapter I want to look at some of the customs which are connected with thresholds and times of change in the life of the individual and also at some of the ways people have chosen to spend their leisure time in competition, sports they have played which have helped them to confirm and strengthen individual and group identities.

Though in more developed countries, pregnancy and childbirth are no longer prone to the dangers which attended them even fifty years ago, they are still times of anxiety both for the woman who carries the child and for her immediate family. Popular comedy can be a useful mirror in which we may see many of our worries reflected in a bearable way (so many comedians tell jokes about race, sexual impotence, adultery, homosexuality, the domineering woman) and the father awaiting the birth of his child is a stock comic character. During earlier stages of pregnancy, the same fraught man is often shown exhibiting the symptoms of carrying a child, in sympathy with his wife, and in many parts of the world this tendency has been formalised in the practice of *couvade*, where a man will take to his bed, abstain from certain foods, and mimic labour. In some societies, the expectant mother may be literally 'confined', kept apart from the rest of the community in a special building while her condition persists.

Nowadays, women who want an easy birth go to relaxation classes at the ante-natal clinic but, in the past, when a midwife would attend a birth at home, she might possibly give the mother a specially inscribed belt to make the birth easier, a custom which persisted in Scotland up to a couple of hundred years ago. Rodney Gallop gives much more spectacular precautions from Portugal in the 1930s:

> To ensure an easy delivery a woman may walk under the canopy in a religious procession. When her hour draws near, nine virgins, all named Mary, should ring nine peals on the church bell, holding the rope with their teeth. To hasten childbirth, a good method is to cut a thread of twisted red silk into fragments, and drink these in wine. When the pains start, in the Alentejo a man's hat is placed on the mother's head until the child is born. The anxious husband can be of more use than is usually the case; for he can hasten a slow or difficult delivery by lifting and turning over a tile from the church roof.

Gallop then goes on to talk of the measures which had to be taken after the birth of a child—especially before it was baptised —with special rites for the water in which it was first washed, the sewing of garlic into its clothes and fastening of rue and rosemary on its bed to prevent it from being bewitched, keeping a lamp burning constantly in the child's room and many other practices. (It is not just among 'superstitious peasants' that such beliefs prevail. Some fifteen years ago, I knew a middle-aged woman from a Nottinghamshire mining background who believed utterly that if a baby's faeces were fed to the fire the child would become constipated.)

Today when a child is baptised it is still customary to give traditional gifts, such as a silver spoon or a christening mug, and anyone who has had a child will be aware how eagerly total strangers, especially elderly ladies, passing in the street will take a silver coin and press it into a new baby's hand. The Ellis edition of 'Popular Antiquities' notes how, in Northumberland, children 'when first sent abroad in the arms of a nurse to visit a neighbour, are presented with an egg, salt, and fine bread' and goes on to say that:

> It is customary there, also, for the Midwife, etc. to provide two slices, one of bread and the other of cheese, which are presented

to the first person they meet in the procession to Church at a Christening. The person who receives this homely present must give the Child in return three different things, wishing it at the same time health and beauty. The gentleman who informed me of this, happening once to fall in the way of such a party, and to receive the above present, was at a loss how to make the triple return, till he bethought himself of laying upon the Child which was held out to him, a Shilling, a Halfpenny, and a Pinch of Snuff.

Nowadays the birth of a child is most commonly celebrated by the custom of 'wetting the baby's head' where the father, fresh from the hospital waiting-room, makes his way to a pub to buy drinks for, or be brought drinks by, any friend or likely stranger who may be there. In the past, a christening feast was *de rigueur* and the women attending, as well as gorging themselves at the table, were allowed to take away with them as much food as they could stuff into their pockets. These gatherings could be an expensive business for poor people and, on occasion, the guests would get together and take a collection to pay for the expenses of the feast. Sometimes after the birth of a child the father would provide guests with a cake and a large cheese, called 'Groaning Cake' and 'Groaning Cheese' in northern England, and, on the day of the christening, the child was passed through a hole in the centre of the cheese.

When a child goes to a new school for the first time, he or she may be subjected to ordeals of varying degrees of unpleasantness. I don't remember such tests at the schools I attended, but the Opies give a number of instances, including having most of the pupils in a school line up along a corridor to kick a new boy from top to bottom, being rolled down a bank in front of the school, and 'bumping' a child on the ground, once for each year of its age.

New apprentices can be subjected to similar induction rituals, which may include all manner of humiliation. Such 'breaking-in' may not apply just to a particular trade, but to a community at large. I have been told how, a few years ago, the new postman to a small valley in West Yorkshire was deliberately misdirected by some of the local people, so that he took the longest possible route on his deliveries.

In England, we have no particular customs which mark the onset of puberty, though buying a girl's first brassière seems to be important to some people. We do have an 'official' age of adulthood, eighteen years, which is unrelated to sexual development and by which age many young people have either married or are thinking seriously of entering that state. Long courtships are no longer as common as they once were. In the past, when a family depended more on the income of its children to maintain minimum living standards, children were often under some pressure to stay at home and help support their parents. At the same time a good marriage, for a girl at least, might be the only way she could 'better' herself and there were numerous ways in which young women would try to divine when and whom they would marry. Martin Luther noted that, on the evening of 30 November, young girls would take off all their clothes and ask of St Andrew whom they were going to marry and John Aubrey mentions a belief that, on St Agnes Eve, 'you take a row of pins, and pull out every one, one after the other, saying a paternoster, sticking a pin in your sleeve, and you will dream of him or her you shall marry'. This kind of belief still holds among children in some places. In Scotland, at Hallowe'en, girls will stand in turn before a mirror, each brushing her hair three times. During this process, the image of the girl's future husband may appear looking over her shoulder and, if it does, she will be married within the year. Also in Scotland, children place two nuts near the fire, one to represent themselves, the other the person they hope to marry. If both take fire and burn gently together there will be a marriage, but if the nuts flare and jump apart the lovers will argue and separate. Rodney Gallop writes of more elaborate forms of marriage divination in Portugal:

> In the *terras de Barroso* the girls go round on the night of St Peter and in strict silence knock on the doors of nine different houses. They are then convinced that they will marry the first man whom they see from their window before dawn, or (lest the oracle should be too easily discredited) someone like him. In other places they fill their mouths full of water and, hiding behind a door or standing at a window, with one leg in the air, wait till they hear a man's name spoken, which will be that of their lover.

On St Valentine's Eve in the eighteenth century, and for at least two hundred and fifty years before, it was a widespread custom in England for a number of unmarried people of one sex to put an equal number of names of the opposite sex into a vessel of some kind and draw them out one by one; in this way the identity of a person's Valentine was determined and there was a good chance the two might marry. Boys would sometimes wear their Valentine slips on their sleeves and treat the girls whose names they bore. In time, this custom was replaced by the sending of Valentine cards that we know today. Most of the messages in the cards are now innocent enough, mass-produced as they are, but sentiments of a more daring nature have been sent to

113

the loved one. W. Chamberlaine, in *The Gentleman's Magazine* for 1805, tells how, as his family was at breakfast on 14 February:

> ... the two-penny-post-man brought in five letters. Three of these were directed to the young ladies; the other two were on business, to myself. My eldest daughter who never receives any letter which she would wish to conceal from her parents, finding that her billet contained what appeared to be Poetry, began to read it to us; but she fortunately had not gone beyond the second line, when I recollected (from having heard of them in my boyish days) what the sequel was; and, snatching, as quick as lightning, the abominable Valentine from her hands before she could possibly arrive at the meaning, threw it upon the fire, congratulating my daughter on having escaped reading the most horrid obscenity that depravity could invent.
>
> A young lady, an inmate in my house, over whom I had not the same authority as over my own daughter, had by this time opened her packet of painted trumpery; and began to read the verses aloud. No sooner heard I the first line than I knew it to contain ribaldry more shockingly indecent, if possible, than the former; I therefore made free to snatch that one also out of the reader's hand, assuring my young friend that, if she had gone to the end of it, she never could again have looked me, or either of the young gentlemen who were then sitting at the table with us, in the face.
>
> The third was then handed to me by my youngest daughter unopened. This was also a Valentine, but contained only a few innocent lines.

Mr Chamberlaine does not, of course, tell us the words of these shocking verses, though they would probably be considered fairly harmless in the late twentieth century. The Opies give some typical rhymes, all of them innocuous, but, by chance, I did come across some Valentine rhymes of a more *risqué* nature. I was looking around a chapel which was up for sale in Sowerby Bridge, in West Yorkshire. It was an impressive building, with a tiered gallery, and also, set as it was by the River Calder, it had the distinction of possessing a water-powered organ which was in the process of being dismantled and transferred to another chapel nearby. While standing in the lobby waiting for the caretaker, I idly lifted the lid of an old desk and found inside fragments of a torn Valentine card. When pieced together the card was still incomplete, but it was possible to make out a good proportion of what the anonymous writer—'your Secret Admirer'—had inscribed in a rounded childish hand. Most of the verses were of the sugary 'Roses are red, violets are blue' variety, but two were plainly intended to be more daring. The first was straightforward enough:

I love you in blue
I love you in red,
But best of all,
I love you in bed.

The second was more of a tease:

I love you, I love you,
I love you almighty,
I wish your pyjamas,
Were next to my nightie,
Don't be mistaken,
Don't be misled,
I mean on the clothes line,
And not on the bed.

Perhaps these were the kind of lines to which Mr Chamber-laine objected, though in this case the writer was presumably a girl, judging from the reference to the writer's nightie and the fact that, in one of the rhymes, the recipient was named as Gary.

Valentines are one of many ways for young people, who may initially be shy, to communicate feelings of affection or attraction to each other. Actual physical contact which, for some, may be beyond the bounds of spontaneous possibility, can be provided by social functions such as dances. Today many liaisons are formed in discotheques (where, paradoxically, the dancers do not necessarily touch). Two hundred years ago at the Christmas dances the process of matchmaking was much more formalised. In *The History and Description of the Isle of Man*, published in 1744, George Waldron tells how the pairing-off was accomplished:

There is not a barn unoccupied the whole twelve days, every parish hiring fiddlers at the public charge. On Twelfth Day the fiddler lays his head in some one of the wenches' laps, and a third person asks who such a maid or such a maid shall marry, naming the girls then present one after another; to which he answers according to his own whim, or agreeable to the intimacies he has taken notice of during this time of merriment. But whatever he says is as absolutely depended on as an oracle; and if he happen to couple two people who have an aversion to each other, tears and vexation succeed the mirth. This they call cutting off the fiddler's head; for after this he is dead for the whole year.

Young people often become obsessed with the preservation or loss of their own virginity. In the west of Scotland, for instance, a girl would go and pull three oat-stalks at random from a stack.

115

If the third stalk did not have a top to it she would not be a virgin by the time she got married. At least until the end of the eighteenth century, it was common to find hooped garlands, gloves cut from white paper and other ornaments hanging in English churches to commemorate the deaths of boys and girls who had died in a virgin state. When older people died unmarried, however, the community's attitude towards their self-imposed sterility or barrenness could be quite different, so that, in Wales, the graves of old maids and bachelors might be sown, for humorous effect, with thistles, nettles and other unromantic plants. The Portuguese girl who dies a virgin has a particularly hard time, since she cannot enter Heaven as a maiden. To do so she must first be deflowered by St Hilary who lies in wait for her *en route* to the celestial city.

Marriage is still tremendously important for many people and the notion persists that, whatever the ultimate consequences will be, your wedding should be 'the most wonderful day of your life', enshrined in a special photograph album and sometimes on magnetic tape, and remembered by friends and relatives as a day when everyone let their hair down and drank and ate up to, and often beyond, capacity. In a closely knit community, a wedding can involve many members of that community and children have been quick to take advantage of the general spirit of euphoria to beg favours. Until at least the 1940s, children in south Wales used to bar the road in front of a wedding car with rope and would not allow the party to pass until they had received money. The same practice was observed in the village of Midgley in the Yorkshire Pennines about seventy years ago. In the north of Frisia, in Germany, newly married couples are sometimes kept out of their houses by an old 'witch' (generally a neighbour or the person who cooked the wedding dinner) and are not allowed to enter until they have vowed to make their marriage a good one; while in parts of northern Eifel, neighbours barricade a couple's house and will not let them through until the couple have given them all a drink. Rodney Gallop says of Jarmelo, in Portugal, 'the way [of the bridal procession] is barred with ribbons or cords stretched across the road, which can only be passed on payment of a forfeit'.

Before a marriage, especially one in which a whole family is involved, elaborate preparations are made. The bride's dress is particularly important and families which cannot afford to have one specially made will often buy a second-hand gown rather than go without. People about to be married may have to go through a variety of ceremonies with their work-mates. They may receive a special present towards whose cost everyone has contributed. A man may be given a 'stag' night before the wedding, one last evening of drinking and adolescent foolery before his new way of life begins, or, more pointedly, his friends may remove his trousers, black his face, hang L-plates round his neck and so on, a humorous warning that he is about to enter an unfamiliar state with which he may find it hard to cope.

For families, weddings are often a mark of status. This is quite apparent from the opulence of a royal marriage through to the marriage where parents have saved for years to make sure their daughter gets a good wedding. Not long ago in England, before hire purchase and high wages made the acquisition of material goods comparatively easy, many people thought it wrong for a couple to get married unless they already possessed what were considered to be the basic necessities. Couples would save, sometimes for years, to buy a three-piece suite, cooker, bed, dining table and chairs, the things needed to 'set up house'. In earlier times, however, it was often impossible for a poor couple to consider paying even for a wedding feast and a wedding could scarcely be contemplated without such a feast accompanying it. Sometimes churches had small houses nearby, equipped with furniture and cutlery, where poor people could hold a wedding dinner, and it was a common practice for the bride to sell ale at her wedding to raise money. These 'Bride-Ales' had a similar purpose to the 'Bidding', a celebration before a wedding to which guests were 'bid' by the bride and groom and were expected to make a contribution, sometimes substantial, to the couple. A writer in *The Gentleman's Magazine* for May 1784, speaking of south Wales, tells how gifts at a bidding would range from:

> ... a Cow or Calf down to Half-a-crown or a Shilling. An account of each is kept, and if the young couple do well, it is expected that they should give as much at any future bidding of their generous guests. I have frequently known of 50 *l.* being thus collected, and have heard of *a bidding* which produced even a hundred.

A similar system of reciprocation existed in Sweden and was also the basis of the Penny Weddings which were common in Scotland. The volume of *The Statistical Account of Scotland*, published in 1795, describes how the custom operated in the county of Ross:

> Marriages in this place are generally conducted in the style of *Penny Weddings*. Little other fare is provided except bread, ale, and whiskey. The relatives, who assemble in the morning, are entertained with a dram and a drink gratis. But, after the ceremony is performed, every man pays for his drink. The neighbours then convene in great numbers. A fiddler or two, with perhaps a

Penny Wedding in Scotland.
Based on the painting The Penny
Wedding *by Sir David Wilkie,*
completed for the Prince Regent
in 1818.

boy to scrape on an old violoncello, are engaged. A barn is allotted for the dancing, and a house for drinking. And thus they make merry for two or three days, till Saturday-night. On Sabbath, after returning from church, the married couple give a sort of dinner or entertainment to the present friends on both sides. So that these weddings, on the whole, bring little gain or loss to the parties.

In the sixteenth century, as today, weddings were more occasions for enjoyment than for solemn religious rites. *The Christen State of Matrimony*, published in London in 1543, tells how:

Early in the mornyng the Weddyng people begynne to excead in superfluous eatyng and drinkyng, whereof they spytte untyll the halfe Sermon be done, and when they come to the preachynge they are halfe droncke, some all together. Therefore regard they neyther the prechyng nor prayer, but stond there only because of the custome. Such folkes also do come to the Churche with all manner of pompe and pride, and gorgiousnes of rayment and jewels. They come *with a great noyse of* HARPES, LUTES, KYTTES, BASENS, and DROMMES, wherewyth they trouble the whole Church and hyndre them in matters pertayninge to God. And even as they come to the Churche, *so they go from the Churche agayne*, lyght, nyce, in shameful pompe and vaine wantonesse.

One sixteenth-century priest was even said to contribute to the merriment by going to fetch the couple to be married from their house and preceding them to the Church playing his bagpipes. Then he would place the pipes on the altar while he conducted the service and afterwards pipe husband and wife back home again.

Like Carnival, Mischief Nights and the Christmas office party, wedding celebrations are one of those times where people are allowed special licence to act in a more uninhibited way than usual. According to Rodney Gallop, explosives were a common feature of Portuguese weddings. If the bride was known to be a virgin, muskets were fired and rockets set off, in addition to the usual consumption of huge amounts of food and drink:

> At a wedding at Penedones (Barroso) in 1874, four calves and three pipes of wine were consumed and no less than four hundred kilogrammes of gun powder were expended.

Weddings provided an opportunity for games, too. Some were directly linked with the occasion. One popular sport among the young men at a wedding was stealing the bride's garter. The 1841 edition of 'Popular Antiquities' claims that this was done:

> . . . before the very altar. The bride was generally gartered with ribbons for the occasion. Whoever were so fortunate as to be victors in this singular species of contest, during which the bride was often obliged to scream out, and was very frequently thrown down, bore them about the church in triumph.

A similar custom prevailed in Normandy and, in Yorkshire, to forestall any fracas, the bride would sensibly hand out garters which she kept in her bosom.

There were sometimes horseback races where young men rode to see who would be the first to reach the bride's house— where a bowl of broth waited as a prize—or perhaps for a ribbon like the bride's garter, or to a pole in front of the bride's new house where the wedding cake had been hoisted. In France, at the turn of the eighteenth century, people begged money to buy drink from couples coming out of church and would raise a hullabaloo if they were refused and, in north-east England, in the same century, the newly married pair might be asked by onlookers for money to buy a football. In Normandy, the bride threw a ball over a wall and the bachelors and married men scrambled for it and, in the early seventeenth century, the guests at a Cornish wedding would take on all-comers in a game where one team of between fifteen and thirty players had to try and carry a ball to the other team's goal, which was generally formed by sticking two bushes in the ground eight or ten feet apart.

After their wedding night a couple could expect to be wakened early by music. Sometimes it was sweet, and sometimes it was the more disagreeable concert of the 'rough band', a raucous orchestra which formed most commonly whenever a community wished to show its disapproval of some sexual weakness or indiscretion. In Portugal, Rodney Gallop says that from Trás-os-Montes to the Alentejo 'the chocalhado, a [nocturnal] serenade with prophylactic cow-bells, greets a widowed person who re-marries' and that, in the Sierra de Monfiado, 'the "rough music" is performed at night outside the houses of old women'; the disapproval, he suggests, is of the old women's infertility.

In England, rough music often accompanied the practice known in the north as 'Riding the Stang' and further south as 'Skimmington'. It was generally directed at husbands who had beaten their wives or wives who had beaten their husbands and was not so much a direct punishment as a form of public exposure. In *Folk Lore of East Yorkshire*, published in 1890, John Nicholson says:

> To excite public opinion against a wife-beater, it is customary to 'ride the stang' for him. A 'stee' (ladder) is procured, and a noisy procession perambulates the streets, singing and shouting, and making night hideous with the braying of horns, clashing of iron pans, screaming of whistles, and banging of drums. This must be done on three successive nights to make it legal, or the 'riders' believe they could be summoned for breaking the peace.

The commentary of the picture-book, *The Costume of Yorkshire*, published in 1814, says that Riding the Stang was used 'more particularly in instances where the pusillanimous husband has suffered himself to be beaten by his virago of a partner'. In the accompanying illustration a group of boys is shown with a stang, which is:

> . . . a pole, supported on the shoulders of two or more of the lads, across which one of them is mounted, beating an old kettle or pan with a stick. He at the same time repeats a speech, or what they term a *nominy*. . . .
> With a ran, tan, tan,
> On my old tin can,
> Mrs. . . . . . . and her good man.
> She bang'd him, she bang'd him,
> For spending a penny when he stood in need.
> She up with a three-footed stool;

Riding the Stang/Skimmington, c.1800.

She struck him so hard, and she cut so deep,
Till the blood run down like a new stuck sheep!

There is an account of a similar occurrence, which took place on Shrove Tuesday of 1562 in Charing Cross, where a man was hoisted on the shoulders of four others and led around by the music of bagpipes, shawm and drum. His next-door-neighbour's wife had beaten her husband and he was riding round to expose her. Skimmington was also used to point the finger at a husband who had accused his wife of infidelity and, in this case a woman (not the wife, it seems), might go around, accompanied as usual by a rough band, carrying the effigy of a man crowned with horns.

There is a reference in *'Popular Antiquities'* to a late sixteenth-century illustration of a Spanish custom where a cuckolded man:

. . . rides on a mule, hand-shackled, and having on an amazing large pair of antlers, which are twisted about with herbs, have four little flags at the top, and three bells. The vixen rides on another mule, and seems to be belabouring her husband with a

121

crabbed stick: her face is entirely covered with her long hair. Behind her, on foot, follows a trumpeter, holding in his left hand a trumpet, and in his right hand a bastinado, or large strap, seemingly of leather, with which he beats her as they go along.

It is impossible to say whether the main participants in this custom were the real culprits or merely delegates. Certainly, in some of the English versions, there were ritual beatings (sometimes with a ladle) of the people who were standing in for the accused man and woman.

As people once used, and to a lesser degree still do use, methods of divination to find out whom they will marry, so it was possible to find out who would die in the near future. A popular method in Yorkshire was to go and sit in a church porch on St Mark's Eve between eleven o'clock at night and one o'clock in the morning. You had to do this for three years running and, on the third occasion, the ghosts of those who were to die during the following year came into the church. This tended to have a disastrous effect on the condition of any ailing people whose images had been 'seen'.

On All Saints' Eve in eighteenth-century Wales, after the great Autumn bonfire had shrunk to its embers, each member of a family would throw into the ashes a white stone, marked so as to be identifiable. In the morning, if any of these stones had disappeared, it was an omen that whoever had thrown it in would die before the next All Saints' Eve.

When someone did die it was customary to ring the church bell a specific number of times, so many for a man deceased, so many for a woman and so many for a child. This was called the 'Passing Bell'. Guests were often invited to a funeral by a 'Bidding', when a church official or someone close to the dead person would go round to specific houses, telling the people who lived there that their attendance was welcome. No one who had not been bidden would go. In France, communities had a Bell-man of the Dead and, until the middle of the eighteenth century, the Bell-man of Paris went around, dressed in a deacon's robes, decorated with death's heads, bones, and tears, ringing a bell and crying, 'Awake, you that sleep! and pray to God for the dead!'

A couple of hundred years ago it was usual, as now, to give the funeral guests something to eat and drink. This could take place both before and after the burial and often led to financial hardship for the family of the departed. A Lanarkshire minister spoke with regret of this custom at the end of the eighteenth century:

*17th century Death Crier,
France. From a 19th-century
English engraving.*

. . . no small expense is incurred by the family, who often vie with
those around them in giving, as they call it, an honourable
burial to their deceased friend. Such a custom is attended with
many evils, and frequently involves in debt, or reduces to poverty,
many families otherwise frugal and industrious, by this piece of
useless parade and ill-judged expense.

Often these feasts would develop into lively social gatherings,
but the real fun and games at funerals were to be had at the
'Wake', the night-long watching over the corpse on the evening
before burial. Wakes were once widespread throughout Europe
and from early days the Church tried to stamp them out, though
with little success until comparatively recently. The Irish are
famous for their riotous Wakes and a late-seventeenth-century
account describes how, on such occasions, religious observance
mingled with more secular pursuits:

They sit up commonly in a barn or large room, and are entertained with beer and tobacco. The lights are set up on a table
over the dead; they spend most of the night in obscene stories
and bawdye songs, until the hour comes for the exercise of their
devotions; then the priest calls on them to fall to their prayers
for the soul of the dead, which they perform by repetition of Aves
and Paters on their Beads, and close the whole with a 'De Pro-
fundis', and then immediately to the story or song again, till
another hour of prayer comes. Thus is the whole night spent till
day. When the time of burial comes, all the women run out like

Irish Wake, Defamatory cartoon.
Typically 19th-century English.

mad, and now the scene is altered, nothing heard but *wretched exclamations, howling and clapping of hands*, enough to destroy their own and others' sense of hearing. . . .

These women were professional mourners, paid by the family to exhibit excessive grief for the dead person. Another professional who might turn up at a funeral in Wales and the Border Counties was the Sin-eater. According to John Aubrey (who said that the custom was in decline in the seventeenth century) this character would be outside the house of the deceased as the coffin was carried out and, on receiving a loaf of bread, a maple bowl of beer and sixpence, agreed to take on himself all the sins of the dead person.

In folklore, bees have a strong connection with death. It was a widespread belief that bees would die if their owner did, or that, if bees left a hive, their owner would die soon after. It was also a practice to turn bee-hives round when the corpse was brought out of the house and a newspaper account from 1790 tells how this custom was bungled at the carrying-out of a rich Devonshire farmer:

. . . just as the corpse was placed in the hearse, and the horsemen, to a large number, were drawn up in order for the procession of the funeral, a person called out, 'Turn the bees', when a servant who had no knowledge of such a custom, instead of turning the hives about, lifted them up, and then laid them down on their sides. The bees, thus hastily invaded, instantly attached and fastened on the horses and their riders. . . . A general confusion took place, attended with loss of hats, wigs, etc., and the corpse during the conflict was left unattended; nor was it till after a considerable time that the funeral attendants could be rallied, in order to proceed to the interment of their deceased friend.

It seems plain that there is much in common between many of the customs which are attached to the times when people pass from one mode of existence into another. At such times a symbolic threshold is crossed and the accompanying customs often centre round a real threshold. So, for instance, a new-born child is passed through a hole in a piece of cheese; when a married couple leave the church they are showered with flowers or confetti and, later, they may be barred from entering their new house without payment of a forfeit; the husband carries his bride over the threshold and, in eighteenth-century Holland, people would strew the thresholds of the newly married with greenery and flowers; you wait in the church porch to see the future dead; and when a corpse is carried out of a house the bee-hives are turned round or the Sin-eater takes damnation onto himself. These life-changes often need special people to be in attendance. Their function is sometimes practical, as with the midwife, or symbolic, as with the parson, the professional mourners and, again, the Sin-eater.

Lack of solemnity is another feature these occasions have in common, sometimes, as with Wakes, in the face of church opposition (and dancing was discouraged at weddings as early as AD 364), and though, at least at christenings and weddings, the urge to celebrate seems natural enough, it is plain that the feasts provided could be ruinously expensive and served to raise or maintain the status of a family within the community.

Status can also be increased by successful participation in games and sports. As children we play every day, during school breaks, in the evenings, in the holidays, and compulsory sports are organised for us at school. When we leave school, in most instances, these activities end abruptly. Even pub games are generally given special rooms and monopolised by a restricted group of parties during the course of an evening. The games impulse, though submerged, tends to find outlets in personal relationships at home and at work, sometimes with an unhealthy outcome. Sports, too, are dominated by professional interest and have largely become the domain of professionals. For most people, involvement in sport means watching a match on the television screen in the company of a can of lager and a cheese sandwich. In the days before mass communication, however, people were much more inclined, even in adult life, to get out of the house and participate. Every public holiday seems to have been attended by recreational contests. At the rural Wakes, which were put aside to commemorate the day of dedication of the local church, there was much feasting, drinking and dancing, as well as competitive sports like wrestling and fighting with staves. The games themselves sometimes took place in the churchyard.

Some of the popular games at Wakes, fairs and on public holidays were barbarous: biting the head off a sparrow, for instance, and pulling the head off a goose, where the unfortunate bird, with its neck greased, was hung upside down and competitors rode at it on horseback, grabbing for the head as they passed by.

Horse-racing itself was a popular sport, as were foot-races, and the latter would often be run by a large proportion of a community. In *Sketches of Old Hebden Bridge*, published in that West Yorkshire mill town in 1882, 'Antiquarian', who was born in 1802, tells of one such race:

> So far as I remember, the races at Hebden Bridge were some time in the latter part of the summer, perhaps in August. They were at a set day, for the people knew 'T Brigg Races' were coming on. Just in the same way as those of this generation know when it is going to be fair time. The prize competed for was a Hat for the men and a Chemise for the women, which was given in my time by Mr William Cockcroft of Mayroyd. These articles used to be hung over the doorway outside the White Lion Hotel, on the morning of the races.
>
> The race-course (as I may call it) was from the White Lion Hotel by the way of Commercial Street, to the gates of Mayroyd, and back again. The men would be naked as a rule, though occasionally one with rather more decency would wear a girdle round his loins, but they were often minus even that covering. The women would run in their chemises only. . . . The women's race was discontinued some years before that of the men. The latter would be discontinued, I think about 1820.

Close to Hebden Bridge, in quite a small area to the west of Halifax, the sport of Lark Singing took place in the years before World War 1. These contests were held in pubs and attended by the local Lark Men, who brought with them, in special 'dark-boxes', the lark that they had taken from the nest, reared, and trained to sing. Each lark was exposed to the light in turn, when,

Billetting, Brearley, 1977.

as at dawn, it would give song and the birds were judged on the length and musical quality of their recital. In the same area, another popular Saturday afternoon sport was Knurr and Spell, which is still played today at Norland with much encouragement from the cricketer Fred Truman. The game consists of hitting a small pot ball, the knurr—held off the ground in a sling —with a flat-ended stick, the object being simply to knock the ball as far as possible. It was sometimes called 'Poor Man's Golf'. Prizes might range from a copper kettle to a piano and betting was heavy among the crowd. In the same area a similar, but more skilful sport, was the game of Billeting. The billet was a piece of wood three or four inches long, with a turn at one end giving it a characteristic shape. The player balanced the billet on the end of a stick similar to the spell, tossed it in the air and struck it as it descended. The trick was to cast the billet so that it dropped vertically and to hit it in the very centre of its length. A well-hit billet would skim along just above the ground for a score to fifty yards, then begin to rise like a bird, X-ing in its flight.

Some of the most popular sports were ball games and, specifically, those which appear to be the forerunners of our own varieties of rugby and football. Before the nineteenth century, when the games were standardised into their contemporary forms, kicking a ball about in the streets was a favourite pastime of apprentices, who often still spend their lunch breaks playing football in the factory yard, but mass ball games were also common, played on specific days of the year, in England, Scotland and France. Shrove Tuesday was a common time for these

127

Sedgefield Football scrum, County Durham.

games, though they also took place at weddings, at Christmas and Easter, and on the days of dedication of parish Saints. Participants could number up to two thousand and would be divided into two or sometimes more teams, which might consist of members of different parishes, the opposing supporters of specific leaders, or the married men and bachelors of a parish. It was mainly a man's sport, though women were not barred, and, in at least one place in Scotland, married women competed against spinsters (and the married women always won—or were perhaps allowed to win).

Though it still goes on in odd places, mass football began to die out in the nineteenth century, but before that it seems to have been tremendously popular. Most games took the form of a virtual free-for-all in which the ball was transported by any means whatsoever to one or another goal, which might be a pool, a parish boundary, a mill-wheel or any other suitable landmark. In a Welsh game of *Knappan*, recorded in 1603, as well as the people on foot, horseback-riders took part, defending their possession of the wooden ball with cudgels a yard long. In *Knappan*, the ball was transported by hand, as it was in the Hurling contests of Devon and Cornwall and in the Camp-ball of the south-eastern counties. In other games, including the French *Soule*, which is believed to be the origin of the British equivalents,

the ball was both thrown and kicked. Records of *Soule* pre-date those of the English games, going back at least to the thirteenth century. It was particularly popular in Brittany and was considered to be that region's national sport.

Haxey Hood Game: the Sway. Lincolnshire.

There is an account of a typical game as it was played by school boys on Shrove Tuesday in the eighteenth century, in the parish of Bromfield in Cumberland:

> . . . the foot-ball was thrown down in the church-yard; and the point then to be contested was, which party would carry it to the house of his respective captain; to Dundraw, perhaps, or West-Newton, a distance of two or three miles, every inch of which ground was keenly disputed. All the honour accruing to the conqueror at foot-ball, was that of possessing the ball. Details of these matches were the general topics of conversation among the villagers; and were dwelt on with hardly less satisfaction than their ancestors enjoyed in relating their feats in the border wars.

Still thriving in Haxey in Lincolnshire, and taking place on 6 January, is the Haxey Hood Game, which is essentially very close to mass football. Instead of a ball, however, 'Hoods' are used; either rolls of tightly bound canvas or, in the case of the Sway Hood, leather-encased rope. The Hoods are thrown into an expectant crowd, to be carried either to the holder's own part of

Haxey Hood Game: the Boggans' songs. Lincolnshire.

the parish or, at the end of the day, to the threshold of one of the three local pubs.

One feature of mass ball-games, a feature which was at least partly responsible for their demise, was the violence which attended them. People were often badly injured and sometimes killed, and participants in *Soule* were occasionally drowned. The players at *Knappan* used matches specifically to settle old scores, though open enmity lasted only for the duration of the game and afterwards there was good-humoured discussion of the damage which had been inflicted. Though previous attempts to stamp out the games had been unsuccessful, by the nineteenth century, they caused so much offence and inconvenience to the 'law-abiding', that civil authorities were prepared to use considerable force to end them. In Derby, for instance, in 1846, the football game had developed into a battle between the parishes of All Saints' and St Peter's and it took two troops of dragoons, a large band of special constables and the reading of the Riot Act to quell the violence.

In his book, *Uppies and Doonies*, (the phrase for mass football in Kirkwall in the Orkneys) John Robertson suggests that 'the game may almost certainly be accepted as stemming from a pagan root', and goes on to summarize numerous instances which seem to support the theory that:

> ... *originally football was played not solely as a recreation, but rather as a ritual designed to ensure prosperity and fertility, or generally to work some good for the community.*

Robertson gives cases where communities believed the crops or fish harvest of a winning side would benefit or, for instance, that a girl who kicked the ball would be married within the year, but such instances are infrequent. Emphasis falls strongly on the violence of the games and in many cases their main function may have been that of social regulation, as a general outlet for aggression and to give vent to tensions which had built up between members of a community or of rival communities, as was certainly the case with the Welsh *Knappan*. As long as the authorities were prepared to tolerate the violence, people could get away with acts which, if performed at any other time, would see them in court. It would be worth waiting for the Big Match to exact vengeance with impunity.

Football is still attended by violence, both on and off the field. Supporters take sides, to which they are often fanatically attached, having their respective ritual chants and forms of dress, but they are no longer allowed to take part in the game itself, so the fighting and destruction take place on the way to the grounds and afterwards, in the streets and on the train back home. The mayhem that can result is often seen as a symptom of our society's decadence and increasing lawlessness, but it is no greater, probably rather less, than the violence which accompanied mass football in previous centuries.

Conclusion

T HE INFORMATION IN the previous chapters is merely a small
fraction of the available material concerning folk customs.
A huge encyclopaedia could be compiled from sources
which include private collections, newspapers, journals, books
and oral sources as yet untapped. The reliability of these sources
is also extremely variable, ranging from rumour to well re-
searched field projects which have sometimes taken many years
to complete.

In general, though, we are at least able to say what folk
customs are not. They are not manifestations of any regional or
national characteristics, since many of them are found, comparable in form at least, in different countries often geographically remote from each other. They are not innocuous rural
recreations; many have been attended by violence, sometimes
extreme, and cities and towns have had their customs, some of
which were recorded in times before their presence could be
accounted for by any great influx of labour from declining
country areas to industrialised urban complexes. They are not
pagan 'survivals', which have miraculously lingered on after
losing all meaning and purpose for the participants. Some quite
primitive-seeming customs—for example the appearance of Midwinter horses in parts of the British Isles—seem to have come into
being in comparatively recent times and, judging from the
accounts we have, most had some function to perform, even if
this was a function as mundane as collecting money or food and
drink.

Taking these points in turn, beginning with the notion, still
held by many people, that folk customs are somehow the em-
bodiment of a national spirit or peculiar to the regions in which
they take place, it is quite plain, even from a superficial examination of the information available, that many aspects of customs
are widespread. Spring and Summer poles, decorations with

flowers and greenery, foliate figures, animal disguise, tranvestism and blackened faces, bonfires and explosions—the list could go on —are found in customs from many different countries and from different historical periods. It seems from the evidence that we are dealing with a kind of international sub-culture which has little respect for linguistic or territorial boundaries.

The image of rural innocence projected by the Morris and Maypole Dancers who were sketched in the first chapter is a romantic sentimentalisation indulged in by the Victorians, though its roots may be seen in the responses of some of the earlier antiquaries to the mysterious things they had seen taking place in remote villages. Nor were the customs harmless. To many people, not just the respectable middle-classes, they were a source of inconvenience and annoyance and their riotousness often drew letters of complaint to local newspapers on the one hand and open retaliation on the other. Many customs have enjoyed an ambiguous relationship with both Church and civil authorities. The Church, especially in predominantly Roman Catholic countries, has often been quite happy to integrate customs into its own practices, yet at other times, when Church authority has been threatened, it has been harsh in its condemnation to the point of denying the people who take part in customs the right to enter Heaven. A tiny but pathetic example of such condemnation comes from the Yorkshire Pennine village of Blackshawhead in the early years of this century. There, where the puritanical strictures of Methodism held sway, even over people who were not regular chapel-goers, a girl who was discovered to have been out dancing in another area was 'cried shame on'—she was ostracised by the rest of the community.

Many instances have already been given of the violence of customs and of their consequent suppression by military and police forces. The resulting clashes far surpassed present-day football riots in severity, often resulting in severe punishment or even in death by accident or by execution. *Carnival*, a recent book by the French historian, Emmanuel Leroy Ladurie, tells the story of the Carnival celebrations in Romans, south-eastern France, in February 1580, which ended in a massacre of peasants and the execution of the ring-leaders of a group who had attempted to use Carnival as an expression of protest against the increasing affluence of Romans' wealthy people at the expense of the poor.

A more recent instance, from the pages of *The Gentleman's Magazine* for 1824, shows the kind of response that was likely to greet anyone arrested under suspicious circumstances while trying to earn themselves a little money at Christmas time. The events happened in Ireland, in Westmeath:

A description of *mummers*, desirous of renewing the Christmas festivals, lately presented themselves in the neighbourhood of Williamstown, in the Sister Island; but it appears, instead of inspiring gaiety, they excited considerable alarm. They consisted of fifteen young men, grotesquely attired, in ribands, white shirts outside their clothes, papers and rosettes in their hats, and large sashes round their waists; and one was dressed in woman's clothes; two of them carried swords of a very antient appearance; the remainder had sticks. Being noticed by the police landing from a boat, peace-officer Sharpley proceeded to interrogate them; and considering it necessary to prevent such a formidable body from perambulating the district, immediately despatched a messenger to Mr. Goodison, of the College Street Office, who directed peace-officer Campain and his party to proceed to Williamstown, when they took the whole number into custody as suspicious characters going through the country disguised. They were brought before Mr. Alderman Fleming and Sir Garret Neville, when one of them, Michael Darley, who stated himself to be the king of the party, said, that they came from Raheny, and that they had been out on the Christmas gambols since St. Stephen's Day; that hearing there were a number of gentlemen's seats at the side of the water, he and his subjects undertook a voyage across the bay, to visit the shore of Williamstown and its vicinity. On being asked by Sir Garret Neville where they got the swords, he said he got one from a man of the name of Neill, gardener to Mr. Joy, and the other from a person at Raheny, and that their intentions were entirely harmless; they assembled for the purpose of getting Christmas boxes, according to an ancient custom (in his dominions) at the other side of the water; and that the King and Hector (one of his guards) were always armed with swords. To a question by the magistrates, he said he was an historian, and his fool was treasurer, and carried a bladder fixed to a long pole; the party spent whatever they got in drinking, dancing, and other amusements. They got money from Dean Ponsonby, Dean Gore, and many other gentlemen. 'His majesty' referred to Counsellor Casey for a character. The magistrates, after a severe admonition, had them detained for further examination.

There are special problems attached to the respective quests for the origins and antiquity of folk customs. There seems to be a need among the people who take part in customs, as well as outsiders who compile accounts of them, to believe that the customs themselves are extremely ancient (though the notion of how old constitutes 'ancient' can vary enormously). Such a view permeates popular accounts and from there may return to the 'folk'. The editorial comment in *The Pennine Magazine* for April/May 1980, for instance, refers to 'the age-old pace egging ritual', the folk play which, as we saw earlier, used to be enacted at Easter time, and is still played out by the boys of Calder High School (to whose performance the editorial is referring specifically). Academic enquiry has shown beyond little doubt that the play in this area was a nineteenth-century phenomenon, yet here, in a responsible magazine devoted to promoting a realistic picture of the Pennines in the past and the present, we find this unquestioning assumption that Pace-Egging is something whose origins are lost in 'the mists of the past'.

Another problem which hampers the search for origins is that the further back in time one goes, the less frequently one finds records of customs (though many records undoubtedly still lie waiting in libraries, museums and public records offices to be discovered by historians and folklorists). While it is wrong to assume that, because there are no accounts of a custom before a certain date, the custom did not exist before then, it is equally wrong to assume that a custom is ancient because it possesses certain apparently primitive qualities. An example which underlines the dangers of making the latter assumption is that of the fire ceremony which takes place on New Year's Eve in Allendale in Northumberland, where a group of male Guysers, many dressed in women's costume, carry lighted barrels on their heads from the churchyard to the square, preceded by a silver band, and cast the barrels on to the huge bonfire that stands there waiting to be lit. This takes place around midnight, and afterwards the Guysers go off to take part in first-footing around the area. Venetia Newall, the folklorist, visited the ceremony three times around the turn of the 1970s. She found that the local people assumed, in common with folklorists, that the custom was an extremely old one and had notions that it had originated variously in Cornwall, with the Anglo-Saxons, the Vikings and the Phoenicians. However, when Mrs Newall visited the archives in the offices of the local newspaper, which was founded in 1864, she could find no reference to the fire ceremony till 1883. Then, in an issue from 1933, she finally found an account of how the custom had originated. This is the account, as she gives it in a paper printed in *Folklore* for Summer 1974, and entitled 'The Allendale Fire Festival in relation to its contemporary social setting':

> I had an idea that the late Mrs John Forster possessed knowledge of the beginnings of the affair. On Saturday night, round the bonfire, Mr. J. J. Forster gave me chapter and verse. . . . About 74 years ago Miss Russell, as Mrs Forster then was, let her two brothers out to play in the band on New Year's Eve, she going

shortly after to watch night service in the old Wesleyan Chapel. The night was so wild that the tallow candles to light the music stands, while the band played the old year out and the New Year in, would not burn. Some bright spark suggested a tar bar'l. It was got, lighted and the band played round it. How easy and probably rapid the transition would be to a tar bar'l procession is easy to imagine.

The response to this article by the people of Allendale was swift and angry—as far as they were concerned there was no question that origin was so recent—but the author, the Rev. Joseph Ritson, consulted a man who 'was reckoned the best living authority on local history' and who had been born in 1837, only to find that he had reached the same conclusions independently. What had begun in the second half of the nineteenth century, purely as an expedient measure, had developed rapidly into a fully fledged 'folk custom'. Even if, as seems likely, elements of its make-up were borrowed from comparable fire customs which existed over the border in Scotland, there is no way in which the Allendale ceremony can be characterised as an ancient rite which has lost all its meaning for the participants. On the contrary, Venetia Newall was able to trace its evolution through more and more elaborate 'folkloristic' forms which came to involve a large proportion of the community directly. The barrels, for instance, once fuelled by tar, were at one time hard to obtain and people would steal water butts and feed containers from houses and farms. More recently, however, the contributions of outside industry have allowed the stockpiling of three to four hundred reserve barrels, which are stored in a special building raised by public subscription. Tar is no longer used and the community gathers brushwood to be turned into shavings which are then soaked in paraffin. Special costumes were introduced only after World War 2 (though formal dress was worn before this) and became increasingly popular, and the lady who stitched them together from old clothes was allowed to take part in the procession, though with opposition from some of the men (for whom she refused to make costumes).

The emphasis on increasing community involvement which emerges from Venetia Newall's investigations suggests that, in some cases at least, the seemingly primitive aspects of folk customs are no more than superficial trappings that materialise when groups of people band together under certain circumstances to show their solidarity. In the case of Allendale, the seed incident, from which the present complex of events on New Year's Eve grew, occurred at a time when the region's lead-mining industry was at its most prosperous. Shortly after, in the

1870s, cheap Spanish lead caused world prices to descend rapidly, forcing the English miners to seek other employment, either in agriculture or in the coal fields and the industrial cities. Perhaps this threat to the community had a direct effect on the increasing elaboration of the Fire Ceremony, creating an event which, together with the previous months' preparations, asserted the unity of the remaining inhabitants of Allendale. Certainly the example of Allendale suggests that we should look elsewhere, away from theories of pagan survival, if we want to discover why such apparently bizarre customs come into being. Neither do I believe that Allendale is an exception which proves a rule. The Padstow May Day celebrations similarly provide a focal point for total community involvement, as do the many instances of Carnival festivities which can be found throughout Europe.

Another example of a custom which involves a whole community is the battle between the Christians and the Moors in Alcoy, province of Alicante, in Spain. Mock battles of this kind are quite common in Mediterranean countries which once endured occupation by the north Africans, and, in Alcoy, a prosperous paper-manufacturing town of 40 000 inhabitants, the total cost of the celebrations is somewhere around £500 000. The custom had its origin (for once we can talk about origins with certainty) in the siege of 1276, when the beleaguered Alcoyans invoked the aid of St George and, in the ensuing battle, the leader of the besieging Moors was killed and the town liberated. The first record of the battle's re-enactment comes from the fourteenth century and, by the seventeenth century, the all-male bands, who represented respectively the Moors and the Christians, started to divide into sub-groups, called *Filaes*, who now celebrate their unity with separate feasts before the battle, and between whom there is great rivalry. On St George's Day, 23 April, there are processions of civic, guild and religious representatives through the streets and the day ends with a massive firework display. The battle itself takes place on the following day, when the warriors, elaborately dressed in appropriate costumes, appear in the streets firing muskets and the Christians eventually recapture the huge *papier-mâché* castle which occupies the town centre. Then at nine in the evening, the vision of St George, who rides a white charger, appears on the castle battlements amid a storm of smoke and coloured lights that would not look amiss in a contemporary rock concert, the church bells ring and the assembled crowd sings the National Anthem. The motive behind the custom was specifically stated by one of the participants in a recent television interview. It gave him, he said proudly, 'satisfaction in the heart as a good Alcoyan', a

Jack-in-the Green, inn sign near Exeter.

statement which recalls a comment made by the headmaster of Allendale School in 1971, that the men who carry the burning barrels must be, 'reasonably decent chaps, doing something for the village like playing in the local football team'.

While I would not suggest that all folk customs have existed solely to unify the community in which they take place and at the same time to confer status on certain of its members, it does seem that a custom's meaning is more likely to be found in its social function rather than in the exotic features which have attracted the attention of folklorists. In fact many of these exotic elements are not as unusual and 'out of time' as they might first appear. They are all around us still in various aspects of popular entertainment and recreation, and even in advertising. The Jolly Green Giant, for instance, who resembles the foliate figures of some folk costumes, is used to sell his own brand of canned vegetables. Tranvestism and animal disguise are features of Christmas pantomimes—not to mention the 'drag' artistes who provide entertainment in pubs and clubs; and the blacking of faces (which in earlier times it has been suggested, perhaps correctly to some extent, was done in mimicry of the Moors encountered by the Crusaders) enjoyed an upsurge in popularity in the nineteenth century with nigger minstrel shows which, for a time, were themselves as much the domain of the amateur as of the professional. The theme of death and miraculous revival, common to the Mumming Plays and other customs besides, is explicit in many cartoon films—*Popeye*, for instance, and *Tom and Jerry*—as well as in the professional wrestling ring, where it would not be surprising to find one of the combatants masquerading as the Black Moroccan Prince. The potion which the Mumming Play's quack doctor administers is similar in its effect to Popeye's spinach and to Heineken lager, whose miraculous properties have been demonstrated recently in a series of television advertisements.

There should be sufficient examples here to suggest that many of the apparently archaic aspects of folk customs are, in fact, recurrent features of popular culture and are not necessarily forced to have arisen from any preoccupation with pagan rites or fertility ceremonies. Their significance will always be speculative, why people should behave in certain ways under certain circumstances and why those circumstances arise, but many customs revolve around basic human requirements and pleasures —eating, drinking, simple enjoyment and the need for people to examine their identities, both as individuals and as members of a group—and the customs themselves, however strange, provide a framework within which people feel they can legitimately beg

for money, get drunk, entertain or be entertained.

Abbotts' Bromley Horn Dancers, Staffordshire, 1914.

Finally a word about folklorists and their relationship with folk customs. I would go so far as to say that, in many cases, this relationship is symbiotic. Certainly, if folk customs did not exist, no one would be able to observe and record them—that much is obvious—but it would also be true to say that folklorists have modified the identity of many customs, even for those who take part in them, by treating them as a discrete genre of activities which are somehow different from other human pre-occupations by virtue of the qualities which they have in common (qualities which may in fact be found in other apparently unrelated spheres) and by investing them with notions of primitive origin and purpose which are borne out neither by historical evidence nor by the attitudes of the 'folk' themselves. The 'folk' in turn have been quick to take up these alien ideas for their own, some-times unconscious, purposes, whether to confer status on the customs in which they take part, satisfy or impress inquirers from the outside, or simply to make a little money. Take as an example the Horn Dance, which takes place at Abbots' Bromley in Staffordshire, in September (though it is believed to have been a Midwinter custom in earlier times). A party of six men, who are dressed in quasi-mediaeval costume and carry reindeer horns on short poles above their heads, perform a simple dance around the area. Accompanying them are a musician, a Fool, a Hobby Horse of the tourney type and a Maid Marian, who is a man dressed as a woman. The custom has seen some changes since the first description of it was published in 1686. The man-woman appears to have joined the Horn Dancers in the nineteenth century and the special costumes were first made at the instigation of the local vicar in the early 1880s. Most interesting, however, is a report from 1841, saying that the dancers distributed copies of the original seventeenth-century account of their activities, which was written by the antiquary Robert Plot, who had probably not seen the custom himself. This suggests that, even before the term 'folklore' had been coined, the people taking part in a custom were not only making money out of antiquarian interest (they must surely have sold copies of Plot's account to onlookers) but also had a fixed reference point, a predetermined identity, against which to set their own performances. First the antiquary notes the custom. The information he has gleaned, not necessarily entirely accurate, is then appropriated by the people taking part in the custom, who use it for their own ends, which may result in the modification or stabilisation of the custom itself.

Antiquaries and folklorists have not only fed their own ideas into the 'folk' consciousness. They have also, with their wild speculations, fuelled the superficial sensationalism which is the stock in trade of the popular media. While it may not, as yet, be fashionable to ask the question 'Was God a Morris Dancer?', there has nevertheless been enough talk of Horned Gods, Druidic rites and human sacrifice to prompt some young journalist, masquerading as a folklorist, to investigate the activities of the Abbots Bromley Horn Dancers, the Calder Valley Pace-Eggers, the Padstow Mayers, or any number of other groups in England or elsewhere that take part in similar unusual activities. But she or he will be unlikely to find any pagan horrors among the bonfires and processions, behind the blackened faces and odd costumes; more likely *people*, celebrating the changes in the seasons or the landmarks of the human life cycle, letting off steam, paying tribute to their forebears, losing their mundane identities in drink or behind disguise, strengthening the bonds which hold a community together, making explicit the various divisions within that community and, often, above all, asserting their right to enjoy themselves and express their feelings in whatever ways seem appropriate.

Bibliography

ARMSTRONG, Lucile (1978), Ritual dances. *Folk Music Journal*, Vol. 3, No. 4.

BERGER, John (1979), *Pig Earth*. Writers and Readers, London.

BRAND, John (1777), *Observations on Popular Antiquities: Including the Whole of Mr Bourne's Antiquitates Vulgares*. Newcastle-upon-Tyne. [1810 edition, London.]

BRAND, John (1841), *Observations on Popular Antiquities*. London. [Edited by Sir Henry Ellis.]

CAWTE, E. C. (1978), *Ritual Animal Disguise*. D. S. Brewer Ltd, Cambridge.

DORSON, Richard M. (1968), *The British Folklorists*. RKP, London.

EPTON, Nina (1968), *Spanish Fiestas*. Cassell, London.

FRAZER, Sir James (1907–15), *The Golden Bough*. MacMillan Publishers Ltd, London.

GALLOP, Rodney (1936), *Portugal: a Book of Folk Ways*. Cambridge University Press, Cambridge.

GOMME, George Laurence [editor] (1884), *The Gentleman's Magazine Library: Popular Superstitions*. Elliot Stock, London.

GREEN, A. E. (1980), Popular drama and the mummer's play. In: *Performance and Politics in Popular Drama*. Cambridge University Press, Cambridge.

GREENWOOD, Harry (1977), *Memories*. Arvon Press, Hebden Bridge, W. Yorkshire.

NEWALL, Venetia (1974), The Allendale fire festival in relation to its contemporary social setting. *Folklore*, Vol. 85, Summer.

NICHOLSON, John (1890), *Folk Lore of East Yorkshire*, London. [Reprinted 1978 by EP, Wakefield.]

O'SUILLEABHAIN, Sean (1967), *Irish Folk Custom and Belief*. Dublin.

OPIE, Peter and Iona (1959), *The Lore and Language of Schoolchildren*. Oxford University Press, Oxford.

ROBERTSON, John (1967), *Uppies and Doonies: the Story of the Kirkwall Ba' Game*. The University Press, Aberdeen.

RUSSELL, Ian (1979), A survey of traditional drama in north east Derbyshire 1970–78. *Folk Music Journal*, Vol. 3, No. 5.

SHEPHARD, E. H. (1975), *Drawn from Memory*. Penguin Books Ltd, London.

TIDDY, R. J. E. (1923), *The Mummers' Play*. Oxford University Press, Oxford.

Index

Numbers in **bold** refer to colour plates. Those in *italic* refer to black and white illustrations. Other numbers refer to text pages.